CODEPENDENCY AND NARCISSISTIC RELATIONSHIPS

Discover How To Recover, Protect And Heal Yourself After A Toxic Abusive Relationship In Just 7 Days + Step-By-Step Recovery Plan

Codependency

Healthy Detachment Strategies to Break the Pattern. How to Stop Struggling with Codependent Relationships, Obsessive Jealousy, and Narcissistic Abuse

© Copyright 2019 by _____ - All rights reserved.

The following book is reproduced below with the goal of providing information that is as accurate and reliable as possible. Regardless, purchasing this book can be seen as consent to the fact that both the publisher and the author of this book are in no way experts on the topics discussed within and that any recommendations or suggestions that are made herein are for entertainment purposes only. Professionals should be consulted as needed prior to undertaking any of the action endorsed herein.

This declaration is deemed fair and valid by both the American Bar Association and the Committee of Publishers Association and is legally binding throughout the United States.

Furthermore, the transmission, duplication, or reproduction of any of the following work including specific information will be considered an illegal act irrespective of if it is done electronically or in print. This extends to creating a secondary or tertiary copy of the work or a recorded copy and is only allowed with the express written consent from the Publisher. All additional rights reserved.

The information in the following pages is broadly considered a truthful and accurate account of facts and as such, any inattention, use, or misuse of the information in question by the reader will render any resulting actions solely under their purview. There are no scenarios in which the publisher or the original author of this work can be in any fashion deemed liable for any hardship or damages that may befall them after undertaking information described herein.

Additionally, the information in the following pages is intended only for informational purposes and should thus be thought of as universal. As befitting its nature, it is presented without assurance regarding its prolonged validity or interim quality. Trademarks that are mentioned are done without written consent and can in no way be considered an endorsement from the trademark holder.

Table of Contents

Introduction 8

Chapter 1: Are You Codependent? 11

    What it Means to Be Codependent 11

    Codependency: So What? 13

    Dependence vs. Codependence 14

    Signs You're the Enabler in a Codependent Relationship 16

    Are you in Denial? 18

Chapter 2: Understanding Codependent Personalities 20

    Decoding the Enabler 20

    Understanding the Enabled Partner 22

        Case Studies 23

        Narcissistic & Borderline Personality Disorder 25

    Dependent Personality Disorder 26

    5 Types of Dependent Personalities 27

    Common Wounds of Both Personalities 28

    Understanding the Anxious Attachment Style 29

Chapter 3: For the Love of Boundaries 32

    5 Vital Ways to Build Strong Self-Awareness 33

    "So, Where Exactly Should I Draw the Line?" 36

    4 Questions to Eliminate Guilt Before Setting Boundaries 39

    Essential Tips for Setting Healthy Boundaries Successfully 41

Chapter 4: Developing Powerful Self-Esteem 45
  How High Self-Esteem Can Improve Your Codependency.......... 47
  Quit Codependency with these 22 Self-Esteem Affirmations 49
  8 Exercises for Developing Powerful Self-Esteem 50

Chapter 5: Breaking Destructive Patterns 55
  5 Ways to Defeat Intense Jealousy 55
  How to Break the Pattern of Narcissistic Abuse 59
  The 10 Terrible Habits You Need to Quit Immediately 64

Chapter 6: Detachment Strategies 69
  9 Great Habits that Start Healing Codependency 69
  4 Unique Challenges to Get Used to Healthy Detachment 74

Chapter 7: Personal Space & Self-Care 78
  6 Reasons Why Personal Space Heals Couples 78
  10 Ways to Accelerate Self-Growth While You Have Personal Space 81
  12 Self-Care Ideas to Make You Feel Like a Million Bucks 85

Chapter 8: Healing Codependency For Good 91
  The Lessons that Break Codependency 92
  What to Do If…? 95

Conclusion 100

Introduction

At first glance, codependent relationships look completely healthy. There appears to be trust, care, and closeness – and what could possibly be bad about that? Look a little closer and you'll see there's more than meets the eye. Both partners appear to have distinct roles and you'll notice they seem to be stuck in a cycle. One partner is the carer or the 'fixer' while the other partner receives an excessive degree of support which holds them back from any personal growth. Now that you see it up close, you recognize this unhealthy pattern for what it is; it's codependency.

If you're in a codependent relationship, you'll know this one-sided dynamic well. Perhaps you're the enabler, intent on helping your partner so much that you end up doing everything for them – even allowing their damaging habits to wreak havoc. Or perhaps you're the enabled partner, suffering from an ailment, addiction, or mental health condition, and you find yourself relying on your significant other a lot to help you get through each day. Until now, you've been taught to believe that your behavior is indicative of love, but I'm here to tell you that you are very wrong.

Codependency is a deeply dysfunctional condition. When it takes over a relationship, it can hold partners back from professional success, sever cords with family members and friends, cause deep emotional or psychological wounding, and in the long run, it'll create resentment in the relationship. This may result in the ruin of the partnership at hand, meaning everything they've lost along the way was all for nothing. As soon as codependency is identified, it must be stopped or this immense damage will be caused.

In this book, I'm going to help you put a stop to your codependent ways so you can finally be in the healthy, happy relationship you desire. I'll take you from clinging codependent partners to empowered individuals who are on top of their respective worlds. Even if you've been stuck in this destructive cycle for a long time, I'll show you how to quit it for good.

I am proud to say I'm a recovered codependent. Since I evolved out of my codependent habits several years ago, I've helped many codependent couples break out of their harmful relationship patterns. I know your struggles better than most people. I've been there and I understand the aching to be needed – and how it feels to not know who you are, when you aren't needed. I'm living proof that it gets better and that your relationship can feel a million times more fulfilling, loving, and empowering, if you just have the right tools and information. That's exactly what I'll be giving you. In this book, I'll be sharing all the insights that I learned on my journey from codependent to completely in power. Everything that I learned the hard way, I'll tell you simply so you don't have to make the same mistakes that I did. I'll show you how I transformed my unhealthy, troubling relationship into a powerful partnership that still thrives to this day – even twenty years down the road!

Your relationship is meant to thrive. Soon, you'll finally understand what that really means. You'll no longer feel desperate and exhausted by your partner. You'll know how to meet your partner's needs while also meeting your own. You'll know how to give your partner the absolute best, while also relishing certain rewards for yourself. For the first time, your relationship will have true balance and you'll experience what it's really like to love deeply, and be deeply loved in return.

I've worked with many couples that others deemed 'too far gone' and they've all seen a full recovery from their codependent ways. Those who once felt stuck, now know what it's like to evolve and grow. The truth is, breaking codependency doesn't just change your relationship, it transforms your entire life. People I've worked with continue to reap the benefits of their self-work to this day. The help I offered them is exactly what I'll be giving you in this book.

Codependent or not, let's not forget that we all want to find ourselves in loving relationships that bring joy to our lives. This is a commonality we all share. What makes you different is you've gotten caught up in the wrong habits and dysfunctional patterns. With my help, you'll finally remove these obstacles. You can enjoy all that is wonderful about your relationship, while leaving behind everything that frustrates and upsets you.

Here's the first tip I'll give you: start now! As time goes on, codependent couples become more fixed in their ways, finding it harder to break their harmful dynamic. Each moment you waste being codependent is a moment you waste not living up to your full potential. What are you and your partner missing out on while you cling to these destructive patterns? What wonderful experiences or accomplishments could be yours *right now* if you just made space for it to bloom?

By turning to the next page, you'll have made the first step to reclaiming your life from codependency. This is an exciting time – the end of a dark era and the rise of a new dawn where you'll finally be free from the shackles of codependency. Get ready for the new chapter of your life.

Chapter 1: Are You Codependent?

Codependency is an uncomfortable topic for many couples and this is partially due to a big misconception about what the term truly means. The word 'codependent' is thrown around a lot in the modern world, used to describe any couple that is extremely close or spends a lot of time together. These definitions are, of course, completely inaccurate. Codependency is many steps above infatuation or intimacy. It is far more than just reliance or dependence. True codependence does a huge disservice to both partners in a relationship, keeping them anchored in unhealthy habits that are slowly ruining their lives. It's about time we stopped using the term 'codependency' so lightly. Its effects can be brutal, if left unchecked.

In a healthy relationship, both partners give and take from each other in equal measure. You do this chore, I'll do that chore. You pay for dinner tonight, I'll cook dinner tomorrow. It may not always be as straightforward as this and there may be times when the exchange is slightly off-balance – for example, during times of stress, illness or trauma – but this in itself is not unhealthy. This in itself is not codependency. It's normal to see this fluctuation over time. Life happens and we're not always at the top of our game. During the low points, dependence on our partner or loved ones is completely natural. So, let's consider an important question: when exactly does reliance cross the line? When does dependence become codependence?

What it Means to Be Codependent

In a codependent relationship, two dysfunctional personalities find the ultimate enabler in each other. One partner desperately needs someone to take care of them and the other partner feels their self-worth is rooted in how much they are needed. These two personalities attract each other like magnets. Without self-awareness or a helpful third party, this can make a pretty toxic cocktail – one that's definitely not sustainable in the long-run. The needed partner takes on the role of 'giver' or 'rescuer' while the needy partner behaves like a troubled victim, 'taking' from the other partner and displaying an excessive need of care. The codependent giver responds to this need for care by overhelping or overextending their assistance.

This is different from everyday reliance in an ordinary relationship because codependency allows unhealthy behavior to continue. While it's completely normal to expect your partner to pick up the groceries sometimes or cook a meal when you're exhausted from work, it's not normal when one partner is consistently acting as the helper. At times, the giver may even take on a parental role, constantly making sure their partner is okay and helping them perform everyday activities they should be able to do themselves. The needy partner gets away with doing very little while the needed partner does nearly everything. Both dysfunctions fuel each other.

The term 'codependency' used to refer strictly to the toxic relationships of addicts and their partners, but today, it has expanded to include any relationship where self-destructive behaviors are allowed to continue. A codependency may enable any of the following behaviors:
- **Addiction** to substances such as drugs, alcohol, gambling, or any other compulsive activities causing financial strain and other damage to their personal life.
- **Poor mental health**, especially destructive symptoms brought about by personality disorders or depression.

- **Immaturity** and other forms of irresponsibility, where the enabler feels they have no choice but to accept this behavior because there's no way to change their partner and that's 'just how they are.'
- **Underachievement,** which may or may not be related to any of the above behaviors. The underachieving partner is not pulling their weight financially or giving up on personal goals, and the enabler allows this to continue.

Codependency: So What?

Here's a question I hear a lot: "So what if a couple is codependent? If one partner feels fulfilled as the helper and they happen to find someone that needs to be helped, what's the problem? No one is being forced to do anything they don't want to do! Maybe they're happy this way."

A codependent couple can indeed appear happy, but this brittle happiness rests entirely on their denial. When a codependent partner overhelps their partner, they hold back their loved one from emotional and psychological growth. Destructive behavior is allowed to run rampant. The relationship starts to function like a crutch, where the fragile partner never learns how to take care of their own needs. They no longer feel the urgency to fix their own problems. Instead, they expect someone else to pick up the slack. When a person is treated like a child, they become disempowered and disconnected from their own inner strength. They are not given the opportunity to psychologically mature. This needy attitude affects far more than their romantic life; in fact, it's likely their professional life is suffering too. After all, bosses and coworkers are a lot less understanding than our loving partners!

And matters are just as bad for codependent enablers. They may appear to accomplish more than their partners, but they're also being held back from their full potential. Enablers feel their self-worth is rooted in how needed they are and their ability to help – this is an extremely unhealthy way to determine one's value. Those with this mentality have a hard time recognizing and vocalizing their own needs because they constantly think someone else's needs are more important. Can anyone be truly happy if their needs aren't being met? Many codependent couples stay together for the long-term, but by the end, enablers are often resentful and exhausted by the life they've lived serving someone else, with little care for their own self.

Dependence vs. Codependence

In a loving relationship, it is expected and completely healthy for both partners to depend on each other. This is what being in a relationship is all about! Unfortunately, many codependent couples who fail to see their dysfunctional ways think they're only engaging in healthy dependence. If you're not well-versed in the patterns of codependency, it can be difficult to tell between the two. To help you differentiate between dependence and codependence, let's compare the two types of behavior.

Example #1

Dependent: Partner A is going through a rough time and Partner B feels bad for them. In an attempt to cheer Partner A up, Partner B does something special with hopes it'll make a positive difference. B understands he can't change anything, but he wants to at least bring a smile to A's face.

Codependent: When Partner A starts going through a rough time, Partner B feels he needs to help A solve the problem. Partner B will do everything he can to make his partner feel better. When the attempts don't seem to be working, Partner B will start to feel worthless, like he can't do anything right. Unless he can ease Partner A's suffering, he feels extreme frustration with himself.

Example #2

Dependent: Partner B wants to spend a day in nature alone to destress after an exhausting work week. He tells Partner A his plan and she encourages him to do whatever he needs to do to take care of his mental state. She spends a day enjoying her own hobbies while her partner relaxes by himself. When they reunite at the end of the day, they feel refreshed after some alone time and happy to see each other.

Codependent: Partner B needs to destress alone but he's nervous to ask Partner A in case she takes it the wrong way. When he finally asks Partner A if they can have a day apart, she looks sad but begrudgingly allows him to go. While they're away from each other, they are anxious. Partner B starts to feel guilty for leaving Partner A and he thinks to himself that it was a bad idea. When they reunite at the end of the day, Partner A is sulky and tries to guilt trip Partner B for leaving. Feeling bad, Partner B feels he has to fix it and make it up to her.

Example #3

Dependent: Both partners express what they need to feel valued and taken care of in the relationship. Each person makes their thoughts and feelings known while the other listens closely and thinks of how they can best meet their partner's needs.

Codependent: Partner A expresses her needs while Partner B listens closely and tries to help. Partner A is seen as having more pressing needs since her emotional state is more fragile. Partner B may bring up his concerns, but this gets brushed aside since he believes fragile Partner A has more important needs. Partner A silently agrees that her needs are more important.

It can be exceedingly difficult for people to admit to codependence. The fact of the matter is that codependent partners often have pure intentions at heart; they simply want to help their significant others and ease their suffering. Still, the results are no less counterproductive. In most cases, the dynamic does far more harm than good to both partners involved. If you think you might be in a codependent relationship, it's vital that you recognize this as soon as possible.

Signs You're the Enabler in a Codependent Relationship

The caretaker or 'giver' in a codependent relationship is also called the 'enabler.' This is because, through excessive care, they are enabling their partner's self-destructive behavior. If you tick three or more of the following boxes, then you are most likely the enabler in your relationship.

- You Constantly Give In

When your partner needs or wants something, you always find yourself giving in and doing what they want. Sometimes it will feel unreasonable and you may even resent them for it – but you continue to give in anyway. You end up dismissing your feelings to take care of your partner or keep the peace.

- You Take Responsibility for Their Actions

When a needy partner does something wrong or displays negative behavior, a codependent may find themselves taking responsibility for it. Instead of seeing their partner as the sole person at fault, they will believe they influenced that behavior. Codependent givers constantly make excuses for their partners and they may even blame themselves for it.

- You Perform Simple Tasks They Should Be Doing for Themselves

It's normal to care for our partners, but how often are you required to help with simple tasks that every other adult can accomplish just fine?

Are you the person that gets your partner fed? Do you constantly have to wake them up so they aren't late to appointments? Do you end up finishing the chores that they were supposed to handle?

- You're Always Trying to Fix Everything

You just can't help it. No matter what happens, you're always trying to meet needs that may or may not exist. If your partner isn't feeling his or her best, you feel like it's your responsibility to make them feel better. You may find yourself anticipating their needs and perhaps even trying to fix something that doesn't need to be fixed. In any case, whenever your partner needs anything, you're always there doing everything you can to make it better, even when they're not doing anything to help their own self.

- You Frequently Have to Ask for Your Partner's Approval

For one reason or another, you don't feel like you can do as you please. If you want to make a decision for yourself or have some time away, you feel like you need to check if your partner is okay with this. The reason behind this behavior is likely that you feel your partner may need you and the idea of your partner being alone makes you feel guilty. By getting your partner's approval, this guilt is eliminated.

- You See Your Partner as Helpless

Be honest with yourself here. Imagine your partner being left to their own devices for a whole week. Perhaps you're going away on an important trip to a place with minimal phone reception. Your partner will have to do everything on their own and look after him or herself without any outside help at all. How worried does this thought make you? Do you trust that your partner will be able to take care of him or herself and function properly without you? Will they be able to stay away from their bad habits, eat and sleep well, and get to important appointments on time? If you answered no to any of these questions, admit it to yourself: you believe your partner is helpless.

- When You're Not Taking Care of Your Loved One, You Feel Like a Bad Partner

At the end of the day, you continue giving and enabling because the alternative makes you feel guilty. You worry that if you set any boundaries, this will make matters worse for your partner. You feel that your partner really needs you and the thought of not helping them with everyday activities feels akin to tossing them overboard into the ocean. You are used to providing assistance and when you don't, you feel like you've done something terrible.

Are you in Denial?

One of the major obstacles in codependent relationships is denial. It is a core symptom of codependency. Even with expert advice right in front of you, nothing will help your situation if you can't admit there's something wrong. One of the reasons codependency is allowed to continue is because both partners are in denial about their unhealthy cycle. Before dysfunctions can be treated, it's essential that both partners stop living in denial about their bad habits or the severity of their effects. These are the signs you've been living in denial.

- You dismiss your own feelings and instincts

It's happened before. You've felt something nudge at your mind, saying, "It shouldn't be like this" or "This doesn't feel quite right." Instead of delving deeper into the issue, you always decide to brush this feeling aside. You tell yourself it isn't important or that the feeling is outright silly, even though this isn't the first time you've felt this way. If you often find yourself having to dismiss your instincts, thoughts, or feelings, then there's a good chance you're in denial. If a feeling continues to resurface, chances are that your intuition is correct.

- You're just waiting for change

Perhaps you've admitted to yourself that there needs to be change. What happens after that admission? Do you and your partner take action to remedy the situation immediately? Or do you just sit back and tell yourself it'll change with time? Relying on external influences or other people to change is another red flag you're in denial, especially if you've been 'waiting' for a rather long time. This shows you've given up your power to create change. Instead of making progress yourself, you are waiting for it to fall from the sky. People who do this tend to be in denial about how bad their situation is.

- Everyone sees a problem you don't see

Are there people in your life who insist your relationship is deeply flawed? The more people who have said this to you, the higher the likelihood that they're correct. If you can't see this problem, you're probably in denial about its existence. When we're entrenched in a dysfunctional pattern, sometimes it can be difficult to point it out. People on the outside of your relationship, however, can see the big picture. And the people who are close to you will know you best and what is best for you. If you constantly find yourself defending your relationship to close friends and family, there's a chance you're in denial that what they're saying is true.

Denial protects us from a harsh truth. By pretending not to notice something, we feel there's a possibility we can ignore it out of existence. This could not be further from the truth and in fact, denial can cause more harm than good. If you want to continue healing your relationship, nip your denial in the bud right now. Change only comes when you face reality.

Chapter 2: Understanding Codependent Personalities

What many people fail to realize is that it takes two dependent personalities to create a codependent relationship. These personalities are distinct but equally as problematic as each other. Those on the outside of the relationship have a tendency to blame whichever person is the most needy, but the fact of the matter is it's not just one person's fault. Both personalities carry their own dysfunctional traits, they just manifest in very different ways. When they come together, the worst instincts of these personalities are enabled. One partner's unhealthy behavior is exactly what the other person needs to indulge their own unhealthy behavior. This is how the codependent cycle begins and why it's often difficult to stop.

In order to create a healthier dynamic, it's essential that couples reflect on their individual selves. By now, it should be clear which of the two distinct roles each person in the relationship plays. This identification is step one. When both parties are aware of the role they play in the dynamic, there can finally come a greater understanding of what each person can do to heal the problem. It is important that both personalities are regarded with equal importance. To start making progress, both personalities should be studied and understood. It all starts with you.

Decoding the Enabler

At some point in the enabler's childhood, they were made to believe their needs are always secondary. In early studies of codependency, it was believed that enabling tendencies stemmed from growing up with an alcoholic parent, but today, experts agree there can be many causes.

Alcoholic or not, these issues are usually the result of a needy or otherwise unavailable parent. While it is possible that the enabler was subjected to emotional or physical abuse, this is not always the case. Often, they simply grew up amidst highly dysfunctional family dynamics, and this may or may not involve a physically or mentally ill family member. These codependents did not receive adequate emotional care so they became accustomed to having their needs unmet. Most children grow up receiving a lot of positive validation; in the case of the enabler, they likely did not receive much validation at all. This results in an individual who, by default, does not feel very important. Instead, they've learned to find validation vicariously through someone else.

In the case of a needy or ill family member, the enabler may have had some caretaking responsibilities, thus solidifying their comfort in assuming a caretaking role later on in life. Whatever their childhood story, one thing is absolutely certain: the codependent has been taught their worth and value are directly linked to how much they please others and how well they can take care of other people. This flawed belief is exactly what creates dysfunction in this personality type. In an effort to feel worthy and good about themselves, they will seek out situations where they offer some form of help. The most wounded enablers may even feel that the more lost the cause, the bigger the reward. This can lead them into disastrous relationships, creating severe trauma, and only worsening the dysfunction. Still, many of these deeply wounded enablers continue to try and serve, believing that the problem lies with them and not their partner. It is a vicious cycle that only ends when self-awareness comes.

It's important to note that some enablers act from deep abandonment issues where they feel they must do everything to make their partner happy otherwise they will be abandoned. 'Abandonment' here does not necessarily mean a break-up. If the enabler suffered through the death of a sick parent, they may overhelp their sick partner, fueled by the subconscious fear that they'll have the same experience all over again.

If you're an enabler seeking recovery, it's vital that you figure out where this need to overhelp stems from. At what point in your life were you taught your needs were less important? Who was the person whose needs took priority over your own? Once you've identified this essential detail, you can begin to separate that incident from your current relationship.

Understanding the Enabled Partner

When studying codependent relationships, the enabled individual can be far more difficult to decode. Why? Because, while all enablers possess similar endgames and intentions, their enabled counterparts can have wildly different motives and causes. Many grew up being coddled or spoilt as children, so they started to expect the same treatment from other people close to them. But the flip side is also possible – they may have been neglected as children, causing them to turn to attention-seeking behaviors. If they were coddled as children, it's possible they don't recognize the reality of their situation. They may think it is completely normal to be waited on hand and foot because that's how they've been treated all their lives.

Many enabled individuals suffer from an addiction, a physical ailment, or a mental health condition. Instead of making steps towards recovery, they became far too comfortable or even started to enjoy being in a position where they had to be taken care of. Due to the overhelping tendencies of the enabler, they are never required to help themselves. In a person suffering from a physical affliction, this may mean they refuse to get up and retrieve things for themselves, even if they are fully capable. Or they may start to expect others to cook for them, even if they have the strength and resources to do so for themselves. Or they may take an extended leave from work, insisting they are too sick or unwell, even if all evidence shows they are perfectly fine.

Since their backgrounds can vary wildly, it is important to examine their childhood. Look at their relationship with their primary caregivers. Were they spoilt in some way or were they outright neglected? Here are some case studies to better help you understand the background of the enabled partner.

Case Studies

To protect the privacy of the people involved, no real names have been used.

- Mary remembers feeling neglected in her childhood. Her little brother suffered from a myriad of health complications as soon as he was brought home from the hospital. Naturally, he got more attention from their parents. She remembers being all alone with her nanny for days at a time while her parents stayed at the hospital with her sick brother. Eventually, her brother got better, but the dynamic was always the same, with him receiving far more attention than her. When she was a teenager, she admits to exaggerating symptoms of an illness because she wanted to get more attention from her parents. This plan succeeded. Suddenly, her parents began giving her the same attention they used to only give her brother. Worried she would become 'ignored' again, she continued to act helpless and sick because she learned that this was the best way to get others to care for her. Eventually, Mary entered a codependent relationship. Her partner went above and beyond to help her because he believed she was very ill and unable to look after herself. To break this codependency, Mary had to learn that there were other more fulfilling ways to receive affection from people.

- For as long as John can remember, he was always given whatever he wanted. He came from an extremely privileged family and he was never required to lift a finger to do anything. He didn't even recognize what a position of privilege he was in; he just thought it was completely normal. If he needed something, there was always a helper available or his parents could easily pay for a solution. In addition to this privilege, he was also an only child with no one to fight over attention for. His mother, in particular, coddled him and he enjoyed being coddled. Eventually, he got into a codependent relationship with a person who grew up taking care of an alcoholic father. Naturally, she became John's enabler. She allowed him to do nothing, taking care of his every need while he took care of financial responsibilities with family money, but nothing else. When they eventually had children, John's partner found herself exhausted and stretched thin. He never helped her with anything and instead still expected her to help him too. Since John was very used to a female enabler being in his life, it was difficult for him to realize that he had deep-set codependent ways.

As demonstrated, enabled partners can be raised in wildly different ways. What they always have in common, however, is that they're taught to equate affection and love with being treated as helpless. In Mary's case, she started to feel that the only way to get attention from her parents was by being sick. In the case of John, he felt that overhelping and being coddled *was* love because of how his parents, especially his mother, treated him. At some point along the way, the lines became blurred with their primary caregiver.

To help the enabled partner in your relationship, see if you can identify where these feelings originated in their childhood. Is your partner more of a Mary or more of a John?

Narcissistic & Borderline Personality Disorder

When dealing with Narcissistic and Borderline Personality Disorder, emotional and psychological abuse are usually at work. Individuals with these personality disorders are always in the enabled position, never the enabler. The codependency becomes infinitely more toxic when these personalities are involved. Narcissists feel entitled to an obedient partner and may even enjoy watching the enabler stumble over them, trying to do everything they can to fulfill their every whim. Indeed, an enabler is a Narcissist's perfect partner. The Narcissist wants to feel special and like the whole world revolves around them, and there the enabler is showing them exactly that. The enabler of a Narcissist is often referred to as a 'Co-Narcissist.'

Borderline personalities can be equally damaging to the enabler; they are prone to feelings of betrayal and abandonment. In the Borderline personality, the enabler sees a victim they can finally save. The Borderline personality wants a hero or savior and it comes naturally for the enabler to play that part. Unfortunately, what the enabler fails to realize is that this is part of the Borderline personality's destructive pattern. They will never truly be the hero in the story because the Borderline will always feel betrayed and abandoned over something. The emotional instability inherent in this personality disorder means the enabler will never succeed in their attempt to save. The Borderline personality has issues that are solely their own problem to solve – the enabler must recognize this as soon as possible.

It is much more difficult for someone with a personality disorder to change. Unless these partners are self-aware and committed to self-transformation, there is a high likelihood they will continue to engage in their usual pattern. And with a Narcissist or Borderline personality, this pattern can be highly destructive. If you're an enabler to one of these personality types, reconsider your involvement in the relationship or invest in couples therapy.

Dependent Personality Disorder

The most common personality disorder found in codependent relationships is – you guessed it – the Dependent Personality Disorder. Those with this personality disorder may fall into either the enabler or enabled position. Dependent personalities are inclined to feel anxiety and fear when they are by themselves. Naturally, they turn to other people to fulfill all their emotional and psychological needs. Without approval, validation, or help from other people, Dependents feel like a fish out of water.

At their most severe, Dependent personalities may have a hard time functioning in their daily lives without something present. This can lead them to shirk responsibilities and become completely passive. When left on their own, they can feel extremely helpless. As you'd expect, Dependent personalities take break-ups harder than the average individual. They may feel utterly devastated until they find someone else to take their ex-partner's place. When an enabler suffers from this disorder, they may be extremely competent while in a relationship but feel there's 'no point' if they don't have someone.

This disorder does not just affect the romantic sphere of the Dependent's life. In fact, everyone who knows the individual will experience their dependency. Friends, family, and perhaps even coworkers and bosses will see this side of the Dependent.

5 Types of Dependent Personalities

Renowned psychologist, Theodore Millon, can be credited with identifying the five distinct types of dependent personalities in adults. While all Dependents will share similar traits, each type will display its own unique behavior and strategies for getting what they want. If you believe either you or your partner have Dependent Personality Disorder, see if you can figure out which type they are. It is possible to have symptoms belonging to a few different types but there is usually just one that dominates.

- The Disquieted Dependent

The Disquieted subtype is wrought with anxiety and restlessness. They fear abandonment from the people around them and feel intense loneliness when they are not with a supportive figure. Feelings of inadequacy run rampant and they are often very sensitive to rejection.

- The Immature Dependent

Dependents under this subtype have a tendency to be childlike, especially in the face of everyday responsibilities. Despite being an adult, they will find it difficult to cope with typical adult expectations. The Immature type needs a significant amount of 'babying' as they can be naive and lacking in general life skills.

- The Accommodating Dependent

This type is characterized by extreme benevolence and, as its name suggests, a tendency to be over-accommodating. These individuals strive to please others and will come across as incredibly agreeable. Naturally, they take on a submissive role and reject all uncomfortable feelings. These types may be very gracious and neighborly towards everyone around them.

- The Selfless Dependent

The Selfless subtype bears many similarities to the Accommodating subtype, but there is a stronger inclination to abandon their individual identity and merge it with another person's. When left unchecked, they'll become absorbed by another person and live as a mere extension of them. Of all the types, these Dependents are most likely to appear as not having a personality.

- The Ineffectual Dependent

Like the Immature Dependent, the Ineffectuals do not cope well with difficulties and responsibilities. The Ineffectuals will take it a step further, however, refusing to deal with anything at all that may be uncomfortable. A caretaker is essential for them to function in life. They are prone to fatigue and lethargy. They are unproductive and most of the time, highly incompetent. On occasion, Ineffectual Dependents may even struggle with feelings of empathy and instead be overcome by a general apathy towards their life, including any shortcomings.

No matter the subtype, all people suffering from this personality disorder can get better with therapy and committed self-work. In fact, many Dependent personalities have found healthy levels of independence after sufficient treatment. If you feel your codependence is linked to this disorder, rest assured that this condition does not have to dictate your life.

Common Wounds of Both Personalities

All dependent personalities may manifest varying behavior, but for the most part, they are rooted in similar psychological wounding. With the exception of some Narcissistic and Borderline Personality types, codependent individuals have low self-esteem and strong insecurities.

At the end of the day, both partners feel they desperately need each other in order to feel complete. The only difference is it takes different types of behavior to achieve this sense of completion – a feeling that never lasts long because it is always up to someone else to fill this need.

By nature, Dependent personalities have trouble forming and distinguishing their own identity. They don't know who they truly are and they have a low sense of personal value. When asked about their core strengths, many will find themselves at a loss for what to say unless they receive feedback from someone else. Their flawed and incomplete sense of identity is exactly why they quickly latch onto other people. They see this other person as a kind of mirror image. Any uncertainty they feel inside is solved by looking to this other person and merging with them.

To eliminate the Dependent's tendency to attach themselves to another person, it is vital that they learn some level of independence. They must experience the world without a crutch to walk on their own. Their family, friends, and partners must learn to give them healthy boundaries and a healthy level of support. Without challenges, they cannot improve and grow into their strength. Codependency is a quick and easy way to placate a deep wound, but it is never a long-term or lasting solution.

Understanding the Anxious Attachment Style

When it comes to understanding one's approach to relationships, attachment styles can shed a lot of light on why certain people behave the way they do. Quite simply, our attachment style shows us how we go about getting what we want and the strategies we use to meet our needs. Our varying approaches are determined by our childhoods, specifically our relationship with our primary caregiver. If you had an emotionally unavailable parent or one that abandoned you in some way, this will affect the way you behave in all future relationships.

The Anxious attachment style is one of three dominant styles and is the one most commonly found in codependent individuals. The Anxious type is formed when an individual experiences trauma during the developmental period of their life. For one reason or another, their 'safe space' was upturned or destroyed. Their sense of physical or emotional safety was compromised in a significant way and it may have resulted in a life-altering breach of trust. This traumatic incident likely involved abandonment, violence, emotional abuse, or other forms of trauma.

As its name suggests, the Anxious type has developed a deep sense of anxiety in response to relationships and intimacy. Whether they show it or not, there is a hypervigilance for signs of abandonment fueled by an intense fear of being left behind in some way. These types crave intimacy and may even fantasize about the 'perfect partner' while single. In relationships, they may resort to manipulation or playing games during times of deep insecurity. They are more inclined to be pessimistic, imagining the worst outcome especially in regards to their close relationships.

The Anxious type is most likely to end up in a codependent relationship because they have a tendency to put their partner's needs before their own. Since abandonment is seen as the worst possible outcome, they naturally strive for the opposite extreme. In the eyes of the Anxious type, codependency is a sign of deep love and unmatched intimacy. The idea of anything less scares them. Codependency allows them to feel like they have 'tabs' on everything happening in the relationship. This is a coping mechanism for their abandonment issues.

The closeness of codependency grants them the illusion of having total control.

The most tight-knit codependencies are formed by two people with this same attachment style. It should be noted, however, that not all people possessing this attachment style will present signs of the same severity. As with everything, all people are on a spectrum. Those with severe Anxious inclinations will need to work harder on breaking their destructive patterns.

At the end of the day, whichever type or attachment style you possess, the lessons that must be learned are the same. If you saw your or your partner's behavior reflected in these pages, don't feel discouraged over getting called out. Just focus on the lessons at hand and you'll soon find yourself evolving from your codependent ways.

Chapter 3: For the Love of Boundaries

Whenever the words 'boundaries' or 'limitations' come into the conversation, it is always associated with negative connotations. People tend to think that boundaries will lead to some form of deprivation and that all enjoyment will be stripped from their lives forevermore. This is, of course, a ridiculous notion. Boundaries keep us sane and safe. They are akin to the walls of a house, keeping a healthy barrier between what's ours and what's *out there*. Boundaries and walls don't mean that we live in isolation or loneliness; it simply means we start gaining better control over our thoughts, feelings, and spaces. Without boundaries, the world and our lives would be chaos. Start seeing the beauty in boundaries. Would you want to live in a house with no walls? I'll bet not.

One key thing that all codependents struggle with is – you guessed it! – boundaries. Their tendency to merge identities with another individual means that they no longer embrace their independence. They start to perceive separation and individuality as negative ideas. Boundaries are uncomfortable and difficult to put in place because any separation poses a threat to their peace of mind. They see it as being alone indefinitely instead of healthy and temporary space apart. Whether you realize it or not, your relationship desperately needs boundaries. Avoiding temporary discomfort now could to lasting frustration in the future. Perhaps even a ruined relationship. Many couples who allow this to happen look back in regret, wishing they'd been strong when it mattered the most. Don't let that happen to you and your relationship.

To start healing your codependency, a necessary step is to start working on healthier boundaries and the mindset it takes to make them successful.

5 Vital Ways to Build Strong Self-Awareness

Before boundaries can be established, it's important that you recognize what your needs are and, most importantly, which needs are not currently being met. This requires self-awareness. As a codependent, some of your needs will be difficult to admit to. In fact, you may even find yourself outright disagreeing. Whenever the urges to disagree or fight back arise, consider whether this response is really rooted in your needs or whether you're only reacting out of fear. It is highly common for codependents to fear the challenge of independence. To achieve growth and true happiness, however, it's essential that you embrace this challenge. Self-awareness will keep you grounded and alert about what you need to feel fully satisfied.

1. Write Down Your Thoughts

Try to make a habit of writing down your feelings and thoughts. Notice when an emotion arises and take note of what brings this up. This time to focus on your mind will train you to be more in tune with what you feel and think. Sometimes we don't notice because we never take the time to really experience our inner world. Make sure that whatever you write doesn't fully revolve around your partner. Focus on what *you* feel. Write about other spheres of your life or topics that interest you in the greater world. Feel free to write in a journal or just in a Word document on your computer. Wherever you choose to write, the benefit is the same.

2. Visualize Your Ideal Self

The best part about this exercise is that you can do it anywhere, anytime, and it can take as little as a few minutes. For the best results, however, we advise doing it in the early morning or right before bedtime as this is when your mind is likely to be less agitated. Close your eyes and start to form a mental picture of your future self. What does your ideal self look like? What has he or she accomplished that you're proud of? What are your ideal self's biggest strengths? How does he or she act in the face of life's challenges? Now, imagine that this ideal self is actually who you're looking at in the mirror. You already are your ideal self. Embrace the strengths you wish to have. They are already in you waiting to be unlocked.

Not only does this exercise empower you but it also allows you to see what your true values are. And most importantly, it allows you to reconnect with your dreams and your purpose. Needless to say, while performing this exercise, it's important that you keep all your visualizations strictly about you and not involved with your partner.

3. Ask Someone for Feedback

The thought of asking someone for feedback can seem terrifying but it's one of the best ways to receive an honest insight. Make sure to choose someone who knows you reasonably well and whose opinion you trust. Also, make sure whoever you talk to will be capable of staying constructive. Steer clear of anyone in your life who is overly critical or unkind. You can do this in person, over the phone or even by email. Ask this person what they feel your strengths are and where they think your areas for growth are. When you receive that feedback, think it over. Embrace your strengths and also look at your areas for growth in a level-headed, practical manner. When moving forward with your personal growth, try and work on these areas the best you can.

4. Take Different Personality Tests

Whether it's the Myers-Briggs test, a SWOT analysis, or an Enneagram quiz, try and have fun with some different personality tests. The goal here is to get to know yourself a little better and solidify your sense of self. Not only will these tests give you new insights into your personality attributes, they will also point out strengths you may have never considered before. Identifying your Myers-Briggs and Enneagram type will aid you in putting your needs into words, and they'll give you a much better idea of where you'll need to set some boundaries. If you discover that you're deeply introverted, you may realize that alone time and solitude is very important to you. Or perhaps it's the opposite and you realize it's more social time with friends that you desperately need in your life. Take these newly identified needs into account and plan on making them a priority in your brand new non-codependent chapter.

5. Monitor Your Inner Dialogue

Every single person engages in self-talk and, even if we don't realize, we are strongly influenced by the manner in which we speak to ourselves. Pay attention to your inner dialogue when faced with different events and decisions. When you do something wrong, what does the voice in your head say? When you do something right, do you give yourself the positive encouragement you deserve or do you give someone else the credit? Take note of the patterns in your inner dialogue. Notice when you're being harsh on yourself.

Instead of putting yourself down for failures, try to be constructive and show yourself compassion. If you can, think of a solution instead of a put-down. If you forgot to pay your phone bill again, don't dwell on your forgetfulness. Be kind to yourself; perhaps you've been stressed or working hard at something else. What can you do to prevent this from happening in the future? Perhaps, you could create reminders on your phone or leave brightly colored post-it notes on the fridge. Try dwelling on the solution instead of the problem.

"So, Where Exactly Should I Draw the Line?"

Using the ideas in the previous section, you might have come up with a few ideas for boundaries you can set. I highly encourage you to run with these and make them happen! If you still don't have any clear ideas, don't worry. You're codependent and you may not be accustomed to thinking in terms of yourself yet. Here are some ideas for where you can draw some boundaries:

1. Time Together

In codependent relationships, it's very common for both partners to spend an exorbitant amount of time together. This is a good place to start when you're thinking of where to draw boundaries. If you see each other everyday, suggest spending one or two days apart to focus on your individual hobbies. If you live together, this may mean taking the day out in different areas and only seeing each other in the evenings. If it isn't realistic to spend whole days apart, consider modifying your daily routine so you spend a few hours in a secluded area of the house.

2. Household Chores

It's very common for the enabler to take on most of the household chores. They are, after all, the more active partners in the relationship. A great way to establish more balance in your dynamic is by adding more fairness to your household duties. This aspect of living with a partner is easily overlooked but it is a huge signifier of balance or imbalance in the relationship. If you tend to do most or all of the chores, tell your partner you will no longer bear most of the burden. Insist on doing half of the chores each. If you're inclined to be more gentle on them, you could even let them choose which chores they would prefer to do. Make sure you stick to this new arrangement by giving them frequent reminders or putting up a chore roster.

3. Bad Habits

This is a big one in codependent relationships. The enabled partners always have some bad habit that is creating strain in the relationship. It could be something as major as a drug addiction or something less major like general laziness. Drawing boundaries around bad habits is essential in a codependent relationship, especially if it's affecting you in some way. Be firm with this boundary, but also think of ways you can support them through this boundary. If you need your partner to go to AA meetings, consider being the person to drive them to each meeting. If you want your partner to get a job, help them look for jobs and put together a dazzling resume. If there are little habits that bother you, consider drawing boundaries there as well. Don't like it when your partner leaves his dirty socks on the sofa? Start setting that boundary!

4. Verbal Communication: Language & Tone

Verbal communication is a difficult one to master and it's possible your partner has tendencies that really irk you. Maybe even more than that – maybe you find them hurtful and upsetting. If your partner speaks to you in a way that you find bothersome, don't hesitate to call it out, especially if they call you names, raise their voice, mock you, or belittle you in moments of anger. Boundaries around counterproductive communication styles can be more difficult to implement since these decisions are made in the spur of the moment, but I'm willing to bet that until now you haven't fought back. Just calling it out and telling your partner you will no longer tolerate it can be enough to put a stop to it.

5. Decisions and Making Plans

If one person in your relationship consistently takes on a dominant role, it's likely that person makes most of the decisions. Some of these may include what activities to partake in, what to eat, where to go, and who to see. If your partner tends to get his or her way when it comes to making plans, try and point this fact out. Draw boundaries around how often they can dominate your shared plans. Suggest sharing this decision or allocating certain days to your choice and your partner's choice. And if it's you that tends to dominate, have the strength to create this balance in your relationship. If your partner shrugs the decision off and asks you to choose every single time, insist that they choose. They may be hesitant but later on, knowing they made this decision will empower them in their own life.

6. How to Spend Money

This decision is another big one. A lack of boundaries around finances can lead to a lot of resentment for couples who don't learn to work together. In a codependent relationship, there's a high likelihood one partner is spending more money than the other or putting it towards something that is destructive to their own lifestyle. Perhaps you have a partner that is spending all your money on shopping and you just can't say no. Or perhaps he or she is using it to pay for their bad habits. If money is going towards a counterproductive activity or habit, start drawing boundaries here. There are always better things to invest in. Bring up your future together. Think of all the money you could have saved for a new house, a new TV, or even a vacation together. Come together to draw boundaries on how money gets spent and how much; you won't regret it!

4 Questions to Eliminate Guilt Before Setting Boundaries

Whenever codependent partners are faced with the thought of boundary-setting, they inevitably bring up the guilt they feel. This all goes back to the unhealthy notion that boundaries are unkind. Codependent people feel that this is equivalent to slapping their partner's hand away or telling them to back off. Let's clear this up right now: boundary-setting is not rejection! When done properly, no feelings are hurt and everyone wins. A lack of boundaries can lead to people feeling resentment or frustration down the road – and this can do real damage to a romantic partnership.

While it's completely normal for codependent people to have hesitation about setting boundaries, they need to recognize this feeling must be overcome. If the thought of setting boundaries with your partner makes you feel uncomfortable, that's okay! This is just further proof that you really are codependent. The good news is this guilt can be eliminated with some self-reflection. Now, let's get working!

- "How is my lack of boundaries holding me back from my dreams and goals?

After utilizing the suggestions in the 'Self-Awareness' section, think about the path between where you are now and the goals you want to achieve. Whether you realize it or not, your lack of boundaries is creating an obstacle. How exactly does this obstacle manifest itself? This doesn't have to be your big life dream, it can also be your short-term goals. For example, let's say you've been wanting to start working out so you can get in better shape. If you aren't creating boundaries around money and time, this leaves less available to achieve this goals. If you're buying your codependent partner anything he or she wants, and spending every minute of every day with them, how are you going to afford a membership at a great gym? How will you find the time or energy to start working out? Reflect on how satisfying it would be to finally achieve these goals. Wouldn't it be a shame if you let your relationship get in the way? How will you feel later on in life when you realize your chance is over?

- "In what ways will I feel more positive after I set these boundaries?"

Imagine how it'll feel after you successfully set these boundaries. You don't have to name these feelings if you don't want to. Just experience it mentally and emotionally. Try to put yourself in the shoes of your future self. It could be a few weeks or months down the road – whenever your boundaries have been able to reap their full benefits. If you're setting boundaries to get more time to yourself, think of all the things you'll accomplish with that time. Imagine how it'll make you feel to see how much you've achieved because you had the strength to set those boundaries. If you're considering adding more rules to the way money is spent, imagine having all that extra money in the future. What will you do with it? Think of the many wonderful things you can put your saved money towards! Imagine taking a fantastic vacation with your partner because you were finally able to restrict their terrible spending habits!

- "In what ways will my partner grow if I set these boundaries?"

You think you're helping by not drawing boundaries, but this could not be further from the truth. Let's examine that flawed belief for a moment. What exactly makes you think you're helping by letting them do as they please? Is it because in that moment you're not causing them discomfort or displeasure? Why is short-term displeasure the enemy and not long-term frustration or dissatisfaction? People grow through challenges. As a partner, it's not your job to eliminate all challenges;

it's your job to make sure your partner has the necessary support through their life challenges. Support means staying by their side not sacrificing your well-being.

What will your partner improve through these new boundaries? How will they grow? If you're trying to help your partner quit a bad habit, think of the growth they'll see once they finally let it go. Perhaps they'll have better health, more money, and more time to focus on their goals. They may learn to be more patient, more empowered, and they may even start to be a better partner towards you.

- "How will my relationship be stronger after better boundaries?"

With the answers to all the other questions in mind, reflect on the overall impact these boundaries will have on your relationship. You've now identified the ways in which you will feel more positive and the growth your partner will see; what does this mean for your relationship as a whole? Your relationship may be comfortable now, but what if your relationship was empowering instead? Imagine what you'd be able to accomplish together.

Essential Tips for Setting Healthy Boundaries Successfully

1. Add Boundaries as Seamlessly As Possible

Here's a pro tip for setting boundaries with positive outcomes: weave them in seamlessly and do not make a big deal out of them. A rookie mistake that new boundary-setters make is approaching the topic with a heavy, sad air and infusing too much intensity into the conversation. There's no need to treat it this way! If want to reserve a day each week for working out, just say, "Hey honey, I'm going to start focusing on getting fit. I've been dying to get in shape! I'm thinking of making Saturday my solo work-out day. You're going to love my new hot bod - just wait!" Notice how casual and lighthearted this is. By bringing new changes up this way, it doesn't feel scary and serious. It's just a small new change - no big deal! Your partner is less likely to worry and you'll see for yourself how incredibly normal it sounds to draw boundaries.

2. Use Positive Language

If you're trying to suggest more time apart, do *not* say, "Darling, I think we need to spend more time apart. It's driving me crazy and I can't handle it anymore." This negative and emotional language will worry your partner. Remind yourself that this isn't a negative event, it's quite the opposite. Your relationship is evolving. Be positive and excited for your new chapter. If you're discussing your new boundaries with your partner, infuse the conversation with positive language. Focus on the benefits you'll see instead of how difficult it's going to be.

3. Assure Your Partner

Needless to say, the first conversation you have about boundaries may incite a little bit of anxiety in your partner. Expect this and don't let it discourage you. When it happens, assure and remind your partner that the reason you want these boundaries is because you want to improve your relationship. Why? Because you love your partner and you want to ensure both your happiness for the future to come. When your partner appears worried, continue to bring up this fact. Inaction is a greater signifier of our apathy in a relationship; if you're actively trying to make improvements, this is evidence that you really care about the future of your relationship.

4. Stay Firm & Do Not Waver

Since boundaries are new to your relationship, it's possible that there will be some pushback from your partner. Prepare in advance for how you'll respond. Whatever you do, stay firm in your assertions and do not back down. If you appear ambivalent or uncertain, this will only add to your partner's hesitation. Remain confident and you'll eventually convince your partner that this is the best course of action. If your partner is prone to manipulation or guilt-tripping, make further preparations for these tactics. See if you can guess how they'll resist and come up with an effective comeback. Keep the benefits of your boundaries in mind and do not allow them to pull you back into your old destructive patterns.

5. Do Not Make Threats

If your partner disrespects the boundaries you've aligned, it's important that there are some consequences for this – but only handle this outcome when it occurs. Do not make threats in anticipation of this event. For the moment, try to believe that your partner will take these boundaries seriously. As soon as threats enter the conversation, you start veering off into emotionally abusive territory. It is absolutely essential that your partner starts making changes out of love for you and your relationship, and not fear for the consequences you've threatened them with. Threatening them will infuse a lot of negativity into the situation and it will only worsen the codependence.

6. Emphasize Change on Both Sides

If you want your partner to cooperate, avoid making it sound like they are the only person who needs to change. Remember, you're both co-creating this situation. As we established in the previous chapter, it takes two personalities to form codependency. Even if you feel like your partner has more work to do, it's important that you take accountability for your actions as well. Tell them what you're going to do as your part in this new change. Your partner will be far more likely to respond positively if you make it sound like this is a journey you're embarking on together. Do not pin the responsibility solely on them.

7. Abide by Your Own Rules

If you're going to draw boundaries in your relationship then you, too, must respect them. How can you expect your partner to take them seriously if you don't? It is completely unfair to ask your partner to change and then not do your own self-work. If you're trying to restrict your partner's drug habit, then it's only fair you control your alcohol dependence. A good rule of thumb is to treat every boundary you create for your partner as a boundary for yourself as well. Do not be a hypocrite. Keep the playing field level at all times and listen to your own rules. You help to set the tone for how seriously your boundaries can be taken.

Chapter 4: Developing Powerful Self-Esteem

A short message from the Author:

Hey! Sorry to interrupt. I just wanted to check in and ask if you're enjoying the Conversation Skills 2.0 audiobook? I'd love to hear your thoughts!

Many readers and listeners don't know how hard reviews actually are to come by, and how much they help an author.

So I would be incredibly thankful if you could take just 60 seconds to leave a quick review on Audible, even if it's just a sentence or two!

And don't worry, it won't interrupt this audiobook.

To do so, just click the 3 dots in the top right corner of your screen inside of your Audible app and hit the "Rate and Review" button.

This will take you to the "rate and review" page where you can enter your star rating and then write a sentence or two about the audiobook.

It's that simple!

I look forward to reading your review. Leave me a little message as I personally read every review!

Now I'll walk you through the process as you do it.

Just unlock your phone, click the 3 dots in the top right corner of your screen and hit the "Rate and Review" button.

Enter your star rating and that's it! That's all you need to do.

I'll give you another 10 seconds just to finish sharing your thoughts.

----- Wait 10 seconds -----

Thank you so much for taking the time to leave a short review on Audible.

I am very appreciative as your review truly makes a difference for me.

Now back to your scheduled programming.

The overall health of a relationship is dependent on the two individuals belonging to it. It is not its own entity. If you're a deeply insecure person, you're going to carry those insecurities into your relationship. If you're jealous while you're single, you're going to be a jealous partner as well. These issues don't just disappear as soon as someone else is in the picture. Expecting a relationship to fix you is another way that codependency forms. Partners cling to each other with hopes it'll diminish their inner turmoil, led to believe it's the ultimate cure. When it doesn't seem to work, they cling harder until the attempt backfires entirely. To be in a healthy relationship, you need to work on being a healthy individual. One way to do this is by working on your self-esteem. Believe it or not, broken self-esteem is often the root of many flawed relationship dynamics. This is no less true for codependencies. The tips and exercises in this chapter will all contribute to a stronger sense of self and more powerful self-esteem. Take the time out to think of you and only you.

How High Self-Esteem Can Improve Your Codependency

Codependent partners tend to be in denial about the connection between self-esteem and codependency. Many insist that their codependency is born out of deep love and commitment for each other, but this is a delusion. Deep love and commitment may indeed exist but many couples are able to feel the same way without resorting to unhealthy patterns. One of the major differences is that healthy couples have higher levels of self-esteem. These are the improvements self-esteem can make to daily dynamics:

Example #1

Low Self-Esteem: You frequently doubt yourself and feel indecisive. This results in inaction about how to go about reaching your goals. You're not even sure if they're good goals to have. Overall, you feel overwrought with skepticism about your choices in life. This is why you rely on your partner to tell you what to do.

High Self-Esteem: When it comes to your goals, you trust that you can find the right course of action. This doesn't mean you won't make any mistakes along the way, but you trust that if you do, you'll discover how to fix the problem and do so accordingly. You listen to your partner's feedback but you never allow it to be the deciding vote, unless you agree.

Example #2

Low Self-Esteem: It feels like you do everything wrong. Every time you try to do something new, it always backfires and fails. You don't believe you have any strong abilities. You prefer it if your partner does everything because you can't do anything as well as they can. You believe yourself to be deeply incompetent.

High Self-Esteem: You may not do everything right all the time, but you know you're still a highly competent person. There's a learning curve for everyone and you always get it right eventually. You are completely comfortable taking care of your own self and are happy to share chores or other tasks with your partner since you know you can handle them just as well. No one's perfect but you know you can do anything you put your mind to.

Example #3
Low Self-Esteem: You're so afraid of being by yourself. This is why you can't implement any boundaries in your relationship; you're terrified it will cause your partner to leave you. Even when your partner does something that bothers you, you bite your tongue and keep your feelings to yourself. You just want to please them so that they stay with you. You don't know who you are without them and you're not sure how you'd go on by yourself. You desperately need them in your life to feel secure.

High Self-Esteem: Of course you love your partner - after all, that's why you're with them! - but you'll be okay if your relationship doesn't work out. You're in the relationship because you want your partner, not because you *need* your partner. You have no problem being honest and setting boundaries with your partner because you know what you need to be happy in a relationship. If your partner isn't willing to cooperate then that's a clear sign they aren't the right person for you. You know your worth and value outside of being in a couple. Your relationship consists of two whole people – not two halves.

Quit Codependency with these 22 Self-Esteem Affirmations

Positive affirmations are a proven way to improve one's self-talk. By reciting empowering mantras, your inner dialogue shifts and all self-sabotaging tendencies can be relinquished over time. To help build your self-esteem and solidify your inner confidence, try and make these positive affirmations part of your self-talk. Continued practice will rewire your brain to instantly feel more personal satisfaction.

1. Everything I need is already inside of me.
2. I am the master of my own emotions.
3. Today I will overcome obstacles with renewed strength.
4. I am my own fortress. I, alone, am in control of what enters and what leaves.
5. I can easily supply whatever I need.
6. I am capable of doing great things.
7. I let go of my past troubles and welcome brighter days.
8. I can stand proudly and courageously on my own.
9. I am open and ready to experience my true power.
10. Every step I take leads me to success.
11. I am fueled by my inner magic.
12. I am inhaling powerful confidence and exhaling self-doubt.
13. I am stronger than ever before.
14. I am whole and I am enough.
15. I am buzzing with brilliance.
16. Everything I touch becomes infused with light.
17. I am an unstoppable force.
18. I am an overflowing cup of love and joy.
19. I am fire and I am blazing ahead.
20. The universe supports me and all of my dreams.
21. Beauty is all around me and I create it wherever I go.
22. Today is the beginning of my best life chapter so far.

8 Exercises for Developing Powerful Self-Esteem

The greatest thing about self-esteem is that it can be built. How you feel about yourself now is not how you'll feel forever. The only reason you have low self-esteem is because your brain is used to creating negative thoughts about yourself – but it is in no way indicative of who you really are. It's time to break the pattern for good and start looking at yourself with kindness. You possess many positive qualities and it's time you start recognizing that.

1. The Journal of Wins

Your days are filled with wins. You may not realize it, but it's true. The reason you don't notice them is because you're waiting for a big win to fall out from the sky, but you accomplish small and medium wins every single day! These deserve to be celebrated too. Thing is, it isn't realistic to accomplish a big win every day. No one does that! To rev yourself up for a big win, start a journal and fill it with your little victories. Every day, list three things that you did right – both the intentional and unintentional wins. Did you make yourself an absolutely delicious sandwich? Did you spend less time on social media today than you did yesterday? Perhaps you gave a stranger a compliment and it made them noticeably happy? These are all wins to be celebrated!

2. Blame the Circumstances, Not the Individual

Whenever we make a mistake, we have a tendency to blame our personality. This isn't always fair. The next time you fail or make a mistake, try blaming the circumstances instead. For example, let's say you forgot to pick up groceries on your way home from work. Instead of calling yourself forgetful or stupid, try calling out the circumstances that got you here. Attribute this mistake to how busy you've been lately and the stress you've been feeling. You would have remembered to do the task if you weren't so tired! It's not who you are deep down inside. Now, it's important to not dwell on the mistake. Start thinking of solutions for next time, should the same circumstances arise.

3. Talk to Someone that Makes You Feel Great

How we feel about ourselves is strongly influenced by the people we're around. If you spend a lot of time with people who speak negatively about you or the world in general, you're going to absorb this negativity into your self-talk. If you can't eliminate everyone that makes you feel bad about yourself, make a point to also spend time with people that make you feel great. Spend time with them without bringing your partner along, if you can. Do they make you feel funny? Smart? Capable? Insightful? Lean into these good feelings and have fun with your new friend. And recognize that you truly are all these wonderful qualities that you feel!

4. Get Physical

Getting physical may sound like an odd way to build self-esteem but believe it or not, it works wonders. When we go on a hike or jog a couple of miles, we are faced with real evidence of our ability to accomplish something. We are simply doing and then succeeding. When we sit and stew in our own thoughts, it's easy for negativity and self-doubt to come flooding in. We need to get in the habit of simply *doing* and then looking back to see how far we've come. When we get active, we can put a distance to our progress or admire the view from our goal. It's a great way to remind ourselves of our power because we are *using* our power to give ourselves proof! The endorphins from getting active and the chance to remove yourself from your routine will also give you an immediate mood boost.

5. Respond to the Devil on your Shoulder

Some of us have an on-going relationship with the devil on our shoulder. It doesn't matter what we do, there's always a little voice telling us we're still not good enough. This voice may even convince us to stay away from any possible risk because we'll fail or we don't have the abilities to succeed. You've likely heard this voice before. However, I'll bet you normally listen and keep quiet when you hear it. From now on, you will not let this voice get away with making you feel bad. Even if it makes you feel crazy, respond to the devil on your shoulder. Fight, if necessary. Ask him what evidence he has to support what he's saying and throw conflicting evidence back at him. Think of how someone close to you would stick up for you in this situation.

6. Stand in a Power Pose

In a recent study, it was discovered that participants who stood in a power pose saw a decrease in their stress levels and an increase in their level of testosterone (which determines confidence). This is no surprise, of course, as body language is a known way of influencing our own state of mind. The next time you feel disempowered, sad, or low-energy, get yourself into one of these power poses for at least two minutes:

- Stand proudly with your legs apart and hands placed firmly on your hips. Make sure to push out your chest and straighten your back.
- Lean back in your chair and put your feet up on the table. Keep your hands folded behind your head and open out your chest.
- Lean back in your chair with your legs spread apart. Drape one arm over something that is next to you (such as a chair) feel free to do whatever you like with the other arm.

Try and avoid low-power poses by steering clear of crossing your arms, folding your hands, or hunching over in your seat. These will have the reverse effect. Choose a power pose and do it now!

7. Create an Alter Ego

Using an alter ego is a proven method for raising your confidence. In a study on mixed martial arts fighters, it was found that their creation of an alter ego helped to make them feel and perform better in the ring. Think of all the qualities you admire and start constructing a character that embodies all of these qualities. You can even think of a name for this character, if you like. The next time you're in a scenario where you feel shy or insecure, play this character. Ask yourself what this character would say if they were in this position and consider what they would do, how they would behave, etc. If you're taking this character out in public, try to not use their false name or give them a whole new life as it may be awkward if people find out you've been pretending. Make sure it's still you, but the 2.0 version of you. For a little extra fun, you can even play pretend that this character has a superpower. But this time, it's very important you don't try to show it off in public!

8. Treat Yourself Like a Loved One

The next time you catch yourself speaking negatively about who you are or what you've done, I want you to hold those thoughts. Now, instead of saying them to yourself, I want you to think of saying them to someone that you love. How would you feel if you heard someone speak that way to your loved ones? If it makes you feel angry or upset, this is the correct response. This should show you that negative self-talk is not the right way to talk to yourself either. If you want to give yourself criticism, think of how you'd give criticism to someone you really care about. You'd make it constructive and gentle, wouldn't you? Perhaps, you'd even take the time to remind them of their strengths. Imagine forming this constructive criticism for someone else and vow to only criticize yourself in this same gentle way.

Another alternative to this exercise is imagining your negative self-talk being directed at your child self. Do you know what you looked like when you were a little kid? A toddler, even? Can you imagine speaking so negatively to that small child? I'll bet you'd instantly start to feel bad. Again, form criticism as if you'd be speaking to this child self. This is the only right way to criticize yourself.

Chapter 5: Breaking Destructive Patterns

Codependent partners put up with a lot from each other and sometimes this includes a lot of destructive tendencies. Due to the clinging and enabling nature of codependencies, these habits and patterns are rarely dealt with in a proper manner. When the primary goal revolves around making your partner stay no matter what, a lot of problematic behavior gets swept under the rug. Then, denial sets in. Partners get too comfortable in the existing dynamic – so comfortable that incredibly unhealthy behavior is allowed to become normal. Chances are that your relationship, too, is filled with bad habits that need to be broken. You may not even be aware of their impact and the role they play in fueling the toxicity of your relationship. It doesn't matter how much work you do on your mentality; if your actions don't reflect that evolved mentality, it defeats the entire purpose of the self-work. There's no better time than now to end your destructive patterns.

5 Ways to Defeat Intense Jealousy

The clinging nature of a codependent relationship means that both partners, naturally, are afraid of the other person leaving them. This can often result in intense jealousy. One or both partners will look at people who they deem potential lovers of their significant other with heightened scrutiny. There's no telling who these 'potential lovers' will be identified as but whoever they are, the jealous partner will pull their significant other in the opposite direction. When jealousy is on overdrive, this can result in the isolation of both partners, since this is the only way they can assure their protection from individuals who make them jealous.

When jealousy and possessiveness are at their worst, there can also be jealousy over absolutely anyone that's close to the significant other in question. This can be friends and sometimes even family. The jealous partner feels the intense need to be the only one and does not want their 'special' closeness to be rivalled in any way. Needless to say, jealousy in any form can lead to destructive behavior, if left unchecked. While fleeting moments of jealousy are normal, they are considered serious when partners start taking action due to their jealousy. This can be anything like stalking this person on social media or trying to limit their time with our partner. Nip jealousy in the bud before it tears your relationship apart.

1. What if Your Roles Were Reversed?

During times of jealousy, we're essentially trying to guess how our partner feels in that moment. We don't have any facts, just uninformed guesses fueled by our insecurities. We're so hung up on thinking of our partner as a distant 'other' that we forget the terrible outcome we're imagining doesn't make that much sense.

Let's say you're at a party and there's an attractive person in the room. You suspect your partner is attracted to them and your mind is swarmed by awful thoughts where they leave you for this other person. Instead of continuing to picture this awful scenario, I want you to imagine a reverse scenario. What if there was an attractive person in the room that you were attracted to? What would be going through your head? How likely do you think it would be that you'd consider running off with this person and leaving your partner? Would you instantly forget your partner right then and there? The answer is probably no. What's more realistic is you'd notice this attractive person for a moment and then you'd move on with your life. This is most likely how it is for your partner as well. The next time you find yourself feeling jealous, ask yourself how you'd act if your roles were reversed.

2. Use Your Great Imagination to Your Advantage

Jealous people usually have fantastic imaginations. With very little information they can go off into their own little world and imagine the absolute worst outcome. The next time you catch yourself imagining the worst, I want you to try the opposite. I want you to use your imagination to think of the best case scenario instead. There's no reason this would be less likely than the worst case scenario! If your partner has an attractive coworker and you're imagining them falling in love while they work on a project together, stop right there and flip it around. Imagine your partner instead looking at this person and thinking about how much better looking you are. This may be the moment they realize 'Wow, I must really be in love with my partner because even though this other person is objectively attractive, I'm not attracted to him/her." What if, instead, your partner spends the whole time talking about you? These possibilities are just as likely. Why does it always have to be the worst?

3. Talk to Your Partner

Sometimes there's no better solution than just talking it out. Be honest with your partner and tell them how you feel about this other person. Jealous people jump to the worst conclusions and it's only when they hear their partner's feedback that they realize what a ridiculous assumption it was. Your partner may be able to clear up that no, he wasn't staring at that person because he was checking them out, he just thought that they looked an awful lot like their cousin. You never know until you bring it up. Your partner will reassure you that everything is alright and you'll quickly have your jealous feelings resolved. Only do this when your jealousy is really bothering you though, and avoid bringing it up every single time. Whenever you can, you should try and handle your thoughts on your own. Don't rely on your partner to fix everything for you.

4. Accept that Attraction is Normal

You could have the most loyal partner in the world who worships the ground you walk on – even this person is going to find some other people attractive. That's just how we're biologically wired. Attraction is completely normal. You can't stop it. As difficult as it is, you'll need to come to terms with this reality. Instead of feeling hurt by this human impulse, see if you can modify your psyche to just see it as a normal occurrence. Everyone feels attraction. Attraction is not a choice, it is just another feeling like hot, cold, hungry, or thirsty. Feelings of attraction are not the same as love and they are certainly not the same as cheating. As long as your partner isn't being disrespectful, it's no reason to punish them.

5. Remind Yourself that Feelings are Different from Actions

Jealous people get hung up on attraction like it's the same thing as cheating or flirting – but this could not be further from the truth. As we established in the previous point, attraction is a normal impulse. When you find yourself resenting your partner over their possible attraction towards someone, remind yourself that this is not an action they are taking. There's a difference between feeling hungry and gorging yourself on a feast. Someone might be thirsty but that's not the same as downing a jug of beer. Remind yourself that your partner hasn't taken any actions so there's no reason to feel upset or jealous.

6. Recognize that Your Feelings are a Reflection of You, Not Them

What people fail to realize is that their feelings about others are not indicative of anyone else's reality. Your jealousy is, in fact, a reflection of your own inner reality and your own insecurities. If you wish you were taller, you'll be jealous of tall people when, in fact, your partner may not care at all about this factor. A key step to defeating jealousy is to come to terms with this fact. Your feelings say more about you than anyone else. If you get hung up on an idea, it's likely to be more reflective of your insecurities as opposed to your partner's actual sense of attraction to someone else.

How to Break the Pattern of Narcissistic Abuse

As we established in an earlier chapter, many narcissists end up in codependent relationships. Narcissists enjoy finding an enabler and unfortunately, many take pleasure in making them bend to their every whim. If you're currently in a codependent relationship with a narcissist or recovering from one, then there's a chance you've suffered through narcissistic abuse. Before we start breaking the pattern, it's important you understand how the narcissist cycle works:

- STAGE ONE - The Pedestal

When a narcissist is getting what they want or pleased with the way you treat them, they'll respond by putting you on a pedestal. At this stage, it can almost be difficult to believe the narcissist is truly a narcissist. They'll come across as sweet and loving, perhaps even attentive, as they try their best to conceal their dark side. For a short time, you'll feel as though you're on top of the world, like your narcissist partner really cherishes you. It's important to remember that they're only being so nice to you because they're getting what they want. Their goal is to encourage you to continue giving them what they want.

- STAGE TWO - The 'Betrayal'

As soon as the narcissist stops getting *exactly* their way, you'll see a completely different side of them. They may start to feel victimized, threatened or just outright offended. Often times, the trigger may seem completely harmless, though you'll start to recognize common triggers each time. It all comes down to what threatens their view that they are the center of the world. This can vary slightly with each narcissist. This perceived betrayal will push them into attack mode and can lead to much verbal abuse, lying, manipulation, accusations, and other forms of emotional abuse. This is where the narcissist is at his or her worst, actively trying to dominate and force the other person into submission.

- STAGE THREE - The Discard

How the narcissist acts at this stage depends on the response they receive in stage two. If they find it acceptable, they'll stop being aggressive. Instead, there may be mind games like the silent treatment. Without being aggressive or overt, the narcissist will start planting the seeds for stage one again. If the narcissist is not pleased with how you responded to them (and sometimes there's no telling what will trigger this) they will discard you, all for not putting up with their terrible behavior. They'll do this while making you out to be the villain while they're, of course, the victim. It doesn't matter how reasonable you are at this point, the narcissist is set on making a dramatic exit. Partners who aren't yet accustomed to the cycle will find this stage very heartbreaking as they may think they are losing the narcissist for good.

- STAGE FOUR - The Return

If you give the narcissist an opening, they'll come crawling back. Once they're done stirring up drama, the narcissist will try and pretend that they never did or said anything terrible. They'll hope that you, too, will try to let it slide. If you forgive them and allow them to get away with what they did, you'll start back over at stage one, where the narcissist will begin showering you in affection again. This final stage is crucial as it determines whether the cycle continues or if it finally gets better from here. It is at this point that the enabler of the narcissist should think about setting down some real rules.

Now that we've established the four stages of the narcissist cycle, we can finally work on the essential lessons all enablers must learn.

1. Understand that You're in Charge of Breaking the Cycle

Make no mistake, if you want to change the way this cycle plays out, it's up to you to take action and demand improvements. The narcissist will not make any changes on their own. They will continue on the same path because it has always worked for them. They do not have a high enough level of empathy to change on their own for the sake of your happiness. Their priority is getting what they want and they will believe this is the correct way until you show them it no longer works. The narcissist will not change – so you must.

2. Never Blame Yourself

Even though your demands are in charge of breaking the cycle, this doesn't mean you should blame yourself if it goes wrong. When your narcissist displays abusive behavior, it is never your fault. Hold them accountable for their decisions. As soon as you take the fall for something that is not your mistake, the narcissist will feel they have won. They will feel victorious in that moment and worse yet, this will encourage them to misbehave in the future. If they know you'll blame yourself and let them get off scot-free, they will continue down this upsetting path. If they made the choice, they alone should hold the blame.

3. Vow to Make Sure Every Violation is Punished

Always remember that narcissists just want to get their way. Teach them that abuse will only get them further away from their desire. Whenever they do or say anything hurtful, punish them by withdrawing from the situation. Before you do, let them know you are angry and that you will not cooperate in any way if they are resorting to abuse. Show them that as soon as abuse enters the conversation, you are not participating. Removal from the situation is usually the best course of action since some narcissists find pleasure in big displays of emotion. To them, this means you care and this emotion can be used against you. Even if the narcissist says something mildly insulting, they'll begin to learn that even this is unacceptable if you stop allowing them to get away with it.

4. Call Them Out on Everything

Using the narcissist cycle detailed above, keep an eye on which stage your narcissist is in at all times. Whenever you notice them making a power move or trying to manipulate the situation in any way, call them out on it. This is frustrating to the narcissist because they always think they're outsmarting the people around them. If you let them know you're aware of their tactics, this will show them their usual methods don't work. By pointing out their manipulative ways, you can corner them into being more honest with you.

5. Understand that Stage Two is Unavoidable

Unfortunately, there's no way to avoid the perceived betrayal when you're dealing with the narcissist. Unless, of course, you plan on letting them do whatever they want at all times. While you can't steer clear of their strong emotions, you can help them find better ways to express these emotions. Ideally, these improved ways should not involve any form of abuse. If the narcissist is having a bad day, then always do what you can to protect yourself from the fallout of stage two. If you're in a fragile place, you may want to get away for a while and turn your phone off. Or perhaps meditate before you decide to talk to them.

6. Implement Stronger Boundaries at Stage Four

The narcissist has some time to calm down at stage three, so by the time stage four rolls around, try and put down some stronger boundaries. This is the stage where the cycle ends and begins all over again. If you want to start with a healthier dynamic, make this clear to the narcissist once the big explosion has finally settled. It is at this point that the narcissist will be most likely to absorb what you're saying. If you're not sure what boundaries to set, consider the following questions: what was the trigger this time? What abusive or unhealthy responses did they display when they became upset? What did you feel most hurt by? Draw boundaries around their abusive behavior and discuss healthier ways they can let their grievances be known. Be clear about what behaviors you find unacceptable at stage two and be firm about how there will be consequences next time.

7. Know that Attachment or Addiction is Not the Same as Love

If you're in a relationship with an abusive narcissist, consider seeking professional help or leaving the situation, especially if you think your emotional well-being is at stake. Unless the narcissist is committed to improving their ways, it is highly unlikely that they'll make lasting changes for the better. Enablers often stay with their narcissist partners as they're convinced the narcissist will change if they just stick around a little longer. Unfortunately, this results in a lot of wasted time and even more hurt feelings. The enablers will always claim to have a deep love for the narcissist - and in some cases, this may be true - but more often than not, the narcissist just has them hooked. Intermittent reinforcement (the cycle of showing love, pulling it away, then giving it back) is scientifically proven to create feelings that mimic addiction. Often enablers are so hooked to the rollercoaster cycle of the narcissist that they mistake this attachment for love. It's extremely important that you make the distinction between these two different feelings.

The 10 Terrible Habits You Need to Quit Immediately

1. Asking Where Your Partner is at All Times

It's normal to have check-ins with your partner but many codependent people take this to a new level. Every hour to every couple of hours, the codependent couple will feel the need to ask the other partner where they are. What sets this behavior apart from the check-ins of non-codependent couples is the frequency with which they happen and the attitude behind them. When codependent couples check in with each other, there tends to be anxiety behind their questioning. They aren't just curious but they *need* to know. The next time you're apart from your partner, see if you can keep check-ins limited to once every four or five hours at the very least.

2. Looking Through Your Partner's Phone

A surprising number of people are guilty of snooping through their partner's phone. Having done it once or twice is not a big deal but it should *never* become a habit. If you need to look through your partner's devices to get peace of mind, your relationship needs a lot of work. If either partner is worried or anxious, the solution should always be to bring it up with your partner so you can cooperate on the basis of trust. If you can't do this, you should learn to let it go by developing the appropriate detachment tools. Snooping through someone's phone is a violation of privacy, no matter how discreet. A major step towards breaking codependency is learning to respect each other's personal space. Stop snooping!

3. Inviting Your Partner to Every Hangout with Friends

There's absolutely nothing wrong bringing your partner into your friend circle. In fact, some of the best times to be had are likely to come about when this happens. No matter how much fun it is, you should always make sure to get some alone time with your friends. To continue having happy and fulfilling friendships, the initial bond should be nurtured – and this doesn't involve your partner. Your friends may not tell you but they, too, wish they could have you alone sometimes. The dynamic changes once someone's significant other is in the room, and although this dynamic may still be fun, there's nothing like getting quality time the way it once used to be. A great way to maintain a healthy level of independence is by nurturing your relationships and friendships away from your partner, as well as with them.

4. Dropping Everything For Your Partner Immediately

There are times when it's perfectly acceptable to drop everything for your partner. If they're having an emergency, then absolutely go and help them – but don't abandon your life for anything less than this, except for rare occasions. If you're about to have a day of important meetings and your partner is feeling sad, wait till you're done with your obligations. Being sad is not an emergency. Your partner should be able to handle their emotions for a few hours. If you're planning on going to a friend's birthday party but your partner has a cold, do not cancel your original plans! When we get in the habit of abandoning our obligations for our partner, we send the message that nothing and no one else matters. This is a highly destructive attitude to take and one that will lead to a lot of regret in other areas of your life. Let professional and personal development be just as important as your partner.

5. Expecting Your Partner to Always Cheer You Up

We can't avoid feelings of sadness, frustration, or even depression. During these low points, our relationship can be a great source of relief and happiness. If your partner does something special for you in your moment of sadness, this should be considered a bonus, not a necessity.

Unless your partner made a mistake which they're apologizing for, it should never be the responsibility of your loved one to make you feel better. It is reasonable to expect that they treat is with consideration, but our inner turmoil is our own to deal with and no one else's responsibility. A major sign of codependency is the expectation that our partner's will fix everything for us. It's essential that you learn the necessary tools to deal with your issues privately. Your partner has his or her own issues to deal with.

6. Saying You're "Fine" When You're Anything But

If you're trying to quit codependency, you need to learn how to talk to your partner honestly. Stop sweeping everything under the rug. This doesn't mean there needs to be a huge blowout or a big deal made about everything; it just means you need to be honest if something bothers you. When we dismiss our feelings, we risk allowing problematic behavior to continue. Furthermore, we raise the possibility of building resentment or dissatisfaction in the long-term. Both of these outcomes with affect your relationship negatively. For a healthy and happy relationship, learn to talk about your feelings in a constructive and open way. A good rule of thumb is to communicate in "I feel" statements as opposed to accusations, i.e. you would say "I feel upset about what you said" instead of "What you said was upsetting."

7. Frequent Interrogations

Every time we interrogate our partners, we demonstrate that we do not entirely trust them. If you have trust issues due to past trauma, there's a way to seek reassurance from your partner without resorting to interrogations. Instead of firing a hundred emotionally charged questions at your partner, try stating that you feel insecure and need them to reassure you. This is a more honest approach to the situation and it is a far more kind way to behave. When we interrogate our partners, this creates anxiety in them whether they did anything wrong or not. Let's not forget that interrogations are meant to intimidate – to extract an answer by forcing someone into submission. If you want to have a healthy dynamic with your partner, leave out all intimidation or scare tactics. This will only make your partner afraid of you and it could backfire on your relationship. Learn to build stronger trust or find kinder ways of getting the response you need.

8. Stalking Your Partner Online

It's no secret that trust is essential to building a strong relationship. For the same reason you shouldn't snoop through your partner's phone or interrogate them, you should also resist the urge to stalk them online. People who do this will frequently check their partner's social media page, keeping up with their latest 'likes,' comments, and shares. This modern-day habit of keeping tabs on our partner can easily get obsessive and lead to suspicions or upsets over nothing. Many codependents will engage in this behavior without even thinking of the deeper implications. Quit the habit of monitoring your partner's behavior. Talk out your issues with them or learn to let go.

9. Making Every Social Media Post About Your Partner

There are many signifiers of codependence that are unique to modern day and this is one of them. If nearly every post on your social media involves your partner then this is a big sign that your identity is highly dependent on them. As we've established, an identity that revolves around another person is a key symptom of codependency. In a healthy relationship, one's sense of self should be clearly defined outside of the relationship. Interests, hobbies, opinions, likes, and dislikes should not be dependent on the other person in the relationship. If you're looking for an easy codependent habit to quit, try this one. Explore your social media presence without it being so closely linked to your relationship.

10. Helping Your Partner with Everyday Adult Tasks

This screams 'codependency' like few other bad habits. It's completely normal to help your partner out every once in a while, especially if you have a little free time, but do not make it a habit unless they're doing something similar for you in return. If you have extra time to make your partner a packed lunch, then sure, why not? Have you made a routine of packing lunch while your partner makes dinner every night? That sounds like a great balance of tasks. But if you're doing this everyday and not getting anything back, then this is straight-up codependent behavior. In all that you do, ensure that you never 'baby' your partner. Do not perform tasks that all other adults are doing for themselves. If you can do it for yourself, your partner can do it for him or herself too. It's time to let your partner be the grown-up they are.

Believe or not, destructive and dysfunctional behavior are not just about abuse. They can also consist of small, everyday habits that appear harmless at first glance. Over time, however, they wear away at trust and the bond underneath a relationship. To make room for growth, start eliminating these harmful compulsions.

Chapter 6: Detachment Strategies

Underneath every codependency is an unhealthy level of attachment. Partners have merged their identities into one, to the point where they no longer feel they have a separate identity outside of their relationship. What's ironic is that attachment is usually formed through an attempt to create a unique identity. However, we only get ourselves further from this goal since this new identity is so interwoven with somebody else.

Not all codependent partnerships will have outright destructive tendencies but the severe attachment is no less harmful to the individuals involved. In order to break the codependency, both partners must learn to find a healthy detachment from each other. Healthy detachment still allows for expectations and dependency, but removes the sense of desperation and helplessness. Codependent people tend to find this idea intimidating because they feel like codependence is synonymous with love – but once they break this dynamic, they instantly feel liberated. Love that stems from want instead of need is far more fulfilling for everyone involved. To discover what this feels like, make use of these detachment strategies for a more empowering dynamic.

9 Great Habits that Start Healing Codependency

You know all about the bad habits that need to be broken – now, it's time to tell you about the great habits that should replace them. Implement these new practices into your daily life to start seeing a healthy detachment from your partner. By absorbing these new ways into your relationship dynamics, you'll immediately start feeling less codependent.

1. Respond, Don't React

Due to past trauma, some of us have certain reactions wired into our brain. Without even thinking about it, we can find ourselves giving into these impulses out of pure habit. For example, if you were cheated on in the past, you may find it triggering if your current partner has a close friend of the opposite sex. Whenever your partner mentions seeing them, you may immediately feel betrayed and angry, even when you have no reason to be. A good rule of thumb to avoid unnecessary upsets is to cut the impulse off before it takes control. Instead of simply reacting out of habit, take the time to really listen to what your partner is saying. Consider if what they're saying is actually unreasonable or if you're just overcome by bad memories. Respond to what your partner is telling you in the here and now, instead of something that happened in the past.

2. Nurture Your Wants & Needs

Don't lose yourself in your relationship. If there are any interests or hobbies calling out to you, why not pique your curiosity? Dive into new curiosities and continue exploring your established interests. Stop suppressing your wants, needs, curiosities, likes, and dislikes. Nurture and encourage everything that makes you *you*. This will strengthen your sense of self, ensuring your identity is still entirely yours even when you're in an intimate relationship. Having different needs and desires isn't just good for the sake of it; it allows both partners separate worlds to escape into so that they can always remember what makes them unique. This way, they never lose their life purpose and stay firmly connected to their essence.

3. Make Personal Space Non-Negotiable

Don't just *try* to get personal space sometimes; you need to make personal space a non-negotiable. Set aside a day or time when you get to have space to do whatever you want – and of course, without your partner. Stop seeing personal space as a daunting idea and start to recognize it as absolutely essential for maintaining your happiness in the long run. See it as a must-have. Even if you think you'll miss your partner, that's no reason to cling and never let go. Why wait till you're sick of them before you have personal space? Missing someone we get to be with later is an incredible joy. It means the love and excitement is still alive. By making personal space a core part of your lifestyle, you'll ensure that this love and excitement stays alive and doesn't fizzle out. Do whatever you enjoy and give each other space to breathe. This does wonders for every relationship.

4. Be Accountable for Your Actions

As soon as you do this, you create an atmosphere of honesty, humility, and courage within the relationship. Being accountable for our actions and admitting when we've made a mistake can be difficult – but it shouldn't be. When we avoid accountability, we are essentially trying to say we are powerless and everything just happens to us – that it's not our fault because we have no influence over the situation. Why is this a good thing? When we're powerless we cannot take action to make things better. We become slaves to circumstance and the whims of other people. This is why being accountable is so transformative. You are recognizing your influence and control, and by doing so, you are also recognizing your capabilities of making things better. When one partner gets into the habit of taking accountability and owning up to their failures, the other partner (provided they are not a narcissist) begins to get comfortable doing the same. A couple that becomes accountable for their separate actions is a strong couple. There is significantly less upset and frustration in the relationship. Instead of needless blame and sour emotions, there can finally be a focus on solutions. The next time you make a mistake, tell your partner you realized what you did, that you're sorry, and you want to improve things next time. Do not play the blame game.

5. Call Out Your Partner for their Unhealthy Behavior

Just as you should be accountable for your actions, so should your partner. Sometimes it's not easy to recognize when we've made a mistake, especially when certain behaviors are routine. In this case, it's very important for the other partner to gently draw it to their attention. If they don't know, how can they improve themselves for the future? If you notice your partner displaying behavior that is unhealthy or even self-destructive, get into the habit of letting them know immediately. It's also essential that you do this constructively and with kindness. If you are angry and abusive, it is likely that they will respond negatively, adding further hindrances to the relationship's evolution. If your partner starts to guilt-trip you for wanting to spend time with your friends, address this codependent behavior. Say, "Honey, I felt like you were trying to guilt-trip me for seeing my friends and it worries me that we're resorting back to our codependent ways. How can we fix this for next time? I'd love it if we could find a solution so I can get some quality time with my friends. It's important to me that I see them sometimes." See, that's not so hard, is it?

6. Determine Your Personal and Professional Goals

Maintain a strong sense of self by continuing to grow and evolve. If you find yourself feeling stagnant or as though your relationship has consumed you, take time to sit down and reflect. Oftentimes we can lose direction because we haven't identified our wants and our goals. Think about what you'd like to accomplish in the near and distant future, then break these goals down into achievable steps. These can be professional goals, personal goals, or both. Is there a skill you'd like to take further? A new milestone you'd like to achieve? Would you like to lose or gain weight? Is there an artistic masterpiece you'd like to complete or at least get started on? There are numerous goals you can set for your life. Choose something that ignites excitement and joy in you. When we establish goals for ourselves, it becomes much easier to avoid codependency since we are instinctively trying to meet our own goals. It gives us something to strive for that is entirely about our own life and not directly connected to our partner. Make sure you always goals you're trying to meet, even if they are small goals.

7. Get an Outside Opinion

In the most extreme codependencies, both partners shy away from speaking to other people about their issues, especially those pertaining to their relationship. They have developed such an intense closeness to their partner that they feel they don't need anyone else. Unfortunately, this also means that when legitimate issues or problems arise in the relationship, they don't have anyone to tell. An outsider's perspective can be hugely beneficial, especially when it comes from a close friend or family member. Make sure neither you nor your partner shut out your respective support networks. They'll be able to tell when your codependency is getting too damaging. Learn to see this as helpful feedback and not just something inconvenient you'd rather not hear. When we're too close to a situation, it can be difficult to see everything as it is. Rely on your friends and family to tell you what you need to hear. Get in the habit of reaching out and maintaining your outside connections.

8. Say 'No' More Often

There's a huge misconception that if we love someone, we should let them do whatever they want. Hopefully by now, you've realized this could not be more wrong. Never saying 'no' to your partner is one of the key things that can lead to codependency. It essentially means you have no boundaries for your partner. When you get in the habit of saying 'no' to your partner, you're standing up for your needs and desires, conveying that they are just as important as your partner's. It is not cruel to say 'no' as oftentimes 'doormat' tendencies can lead to a quiet resentment in codependent partners. By setting boundaries, you're ensuring that you never exhaust yourself by giving more than you have. Down the road, this means you'll be happier, more fulfilled, and far more ready to be a good partner. The kindness you show your loved one will be born out of genuine love instead of necessity and obligation.

9. Solve Problems Together

When someone in a relationship makes a mistake, people tend to oversimplify the solution-finding process. They tend to think, "You made the mistake, so you should fix it. Figure it out and get back to me when things are better." We leave the person who made the mistake to come up with a solution on their own. Many couples believe this is the fair thing to do, but it's far from it. Healthy couples solve problems together. This does not mean both partners are at fault. It shows they recognize two heads are better than one. If you truly want to fix the situation and not just 'get even,' you should work alongside your partner to find a solution. Examine the problem at hand, what went wrong, and what could be better next time. Get in the habit of cooperating instead of making just one partner responsible for change.

4 Unique Challenges to Get Used to Healthy Detachment

If you're extremely codependent, the thought of detachment may sound scary to you. To simplify your next few steps, consider experimenting with the following challenges. These will help you get in the proper mindset for finding your own independence. At the end of each challenge, reunite with your partner and share your different experiences. See if you can have some fun with these challenges!

1. Draw Your Day

You don't need to have an artistic streak for this challenge – in fact, it might be more fun if you don't! For this challenge, both partners should separate for several hours and draw what they see, wherever they choose to go. They can take their pick of anything they see that day – it can be funny, serious, or even surrealist, if they so desire! Ideally, both partners shouldn't text each other except to discuss logistics about where and what time to meet up later. At the end of the day, both partners can reunite and show each other what they drew. If you're a terrible artist, laughing at your bad drawings could make for a hilarious evening. This challenge is one of the best since it allows people to get in touch with their creative side while also getting personal space. And the benefits don't end there! Partners always enjoy looking over each other's drawings and sharing the stories connected to what they saw.

2. Meet in the Middle

If there's an adventurous side to you, try the 'Meet in the Middle' challenge with your partner. Put simply: it requires both partners to explore two opposite or faraway locations and then meet up again halfway. This challenge can be scaled to suit your time frame and budget. If you're not able to travel internationally, there's no need to fret! Each partner can choose a city or town in the country that they've always wanted to explore. This works especially well if the other partner has already been there or doesn't care to go. Once both people have chosen their city or town, they can pinpoint a location that's roughly halfway. After traveling through and exploring separate locations, they can make their way to each other and meet in that halfway spot. If you have a bigger budget, consider doing this with countries. Solo travel is an empowering experience and couples, inevitably, find the 'halfway meetup' to be incredibly romantic.

3. The Gift Exchange

Just like 'Draw Your Day,' this challenge involves a couple separating for a few to several hours. There should be no communication whatsoever until it's time to reunite, later on in the day. The goal of their time apart should be to purchase, create, or just somehow procure a gift for their partner. The target can be one gift or more, depending on their respective budgets. It would also be wise for both partners to decide on a spending limit, so one person doesn't outspend the other. This is a great challenge to start off with since both partners can still feel close to each other in the pursuit of a gift for their loved one.

4. Outside-Inside

No excuses allowed for this one! One person is in charge of 'Outside' and the other is in charge of 'Inside.' For as long as it takes to finish, both partners must focus on their separate tasks without help from the other. Partners can only communicate over logistics or if they're asking for clarification. All other communication must be saved for after the challenge, when everything is complete. Here's a rundown of what each person is in charge of:

Outside - All errands that involve going out such as grocery shopping, sending mail, picking up tools or materials for repairs, refilling the car with gas, depositing a check or withdrawing money for rent, and many others. It can also include household chores if they take place outside, e.g. gardening, yard work, shed repairs, etc.

Inside - All duties regarding the inside of the home and general housekeeping. This includes doing laundry, making beds, cleaning and dusting the home, tidying and reorganizing clutter, doing dishes, and all other home-related chores.

Whoever finishes first gets to have free time to do whatever they want! The only condition? They must stay away from their partner until all chores are completed.

Why not create your own challenge? For the best outcome, both partners should be separated for as long as possible while focusing on a clearly defined goal or enjoying a distraction.

Chapter 7: Personal Space & Self-Care

We've spoken a lot about personal space and self-care, but some of you may be wondering, "What exactly does that entail?" or "What do I do once I have personal space?" If you're at the extreme end of codependent, you may need some ideas for your next self-care sesh. As we've established, this is crucial for maintaining a healthy level of independence in your relationship. When partners continue to practice this in a relationship, they become stronger, more courageous individuals that see more life fulfillment in the long run. If you're intimidated by the thought of having temporary separation, understand that it's only difficult for one reason: you're breaking a fixed routine! It's in no way indicative of the effects it will ultimately have. Destructive or not, patterns are difficult to break – but once you succeed, your life blossoms in ways you could never have imagined.

6 Reasons Why Personal Space Heals Couples

Before you can come up with excuses for skipping the rest of this chapter, let's examine the benefits of personal space. On the days you're overwhelmed by anxiety, when you just want to cling and never let go, turn back to this section. This is why personal space is vital for healing codependency:

1. It Makes You a Stronger Person

When we are given space to do our own thing, we use coping and self-management tools that we stop using in the presence of our close loved ones. If we have a need, we learn to take care of it on our own. We learn to provide our own entertainment. And we can finally listen and assess our own thoughts, without influence from an outside party. That pang you feel when you're by yourself and you really wish someone was there with you – that's your mind refusing to use your own self-management tools. When we have someone around us, we don't have to use them as much. They can help us perform tasks, entertain us, and they provide us with as many distractions as we desire. This feels good in the same way sitting on the couch, instead of going to work, feels good. It allows us to not do any work, but it damages our ability to fend for ourselves and be self-sufficient. If you don't learn to be strong now, it'll be a hundred times more difficult in the future. Personal space gives us the opportunity to self-manage again and this brings a lot of benefits with it.

2. Reconnecting to Our Individuality Makes Us Happier

When we get personal space, we our reminded of what makes us different. Instead of merging with our partner's identity, we remember our own and what exactly makes us unique. When we reconnect with this part of ourselves, we instantly feel happier. Why? It's simple. We all want to feel special. No one wants to feel like they've become exactly like something else. Those who do are under the mistaken impression that merging identities is the cure to not feeling special. This, of course, could not be further from the truth. To truly feel one-of-a-kind and unique, we need to connect to something deep in ourselves. This part of us can only be accessed through sufficient time alone. As much as you love your partner, too much time together can make you forget what makes you different.

3. There's More to Talk About Later On

If you're always with each other, you're receiving the same general experience at the same time. This can be special too, of course; you can discuss events as they unfold around you and enjoy sharing in the same experience. But don't forget, there's also enjoyment to be had in having different experiences and telling the story later on. Two partners that reunite after a long day apart can relay the stories and events of the day to one another, relishing the storytelling and the surprise element that comes with it. When we're always with our partner, we miss out on the fun of catching up.

4. You Can Get Sick of Great Things, Too – Don't Let This Happen!

You may love and cherish your partner deeply. You may even think your relationship is the best thing in the world and you're so meant for each other that nothing can ruin what you have. I hate to break it to you: too much time together can, indeed, ruin it. Let's say you discovered the world's best pancakes. You found them so delicious you decided to have them for every meal. At first, having your favorite food three times a day seemed like heaven – but what about after a few months? Or a few years? You'd definitely start to get sick of it. Eventually, you'd start to crave literally *anything* else. It doesn't matter how objectively good those pancakes are or how much you enjoyed them in the beginning. If you overdo it, you won't want anything more to do with them. The same goes for you and your partner. Without personal space, the relationship starts to feel suffocating. This will inevitably lead to a more strained partnership.

5. It Reminds You of Why You're Together

When we are constantly with someone or something that we love, we start to take them for granted. We get so accustomed to quick and easy access that we forget how special it is to have access at all. Couples that make personal space a part of their lifestyle experience a lot more gratitude towards their partner. When they're together, they're reminded of the joy that their significant other brings to their life. The periods of being apart create a contrast against the times they are together. This immediately highlights the positive differences their relationship makes. In turn, this makes every moment together seem more special. Partners will appreciate each other much more and be happier in the long run.

6. Happier People Create More Lasting Relationships

Codependence is formed when couples are too anxious or insecure to let each other go. Ironically, learning to do so can actually make the chances of staying together (happily) more likely. Consider everything we've covered so far. There will be more excitement, you won't get sick of each other, *you'll* be happier and so will your partner. Two happy, strong individuals make a happy, strong couple. To ensure lasting satisfaction, there needs to be room to grow. By giving each other space, you're allowing each other space to evolve into better selves. Couples that do this thrive better than the rest.

10 Ways to Accelerate Self-Growth While You Have Personal Space

Codependent people struggle to fill their time when they finally have personal space. Many begin to feel anxiety, not sure what to do with themselves now that their partner isn't there. It's helpful to note this only happens because it is a break from their usual routine. It can be overcome with practice. Personal space is a great time to finally focus on self-growth and make strides towards accomplishing your personal goals. Making the effort to always keep your goals in sight will help you ward off your codependent leanings. Consider the many ways you can do this:

1. Learn a New Skill

Is there a talent you secretly wish you had? When was the last time you thought 'I wish I could do that'? A workshop or class is a fantastic thing to add to a schedule and it's a great use of personal time. It can be anything from painting and photography classes to kung fu lessons. The sky's the limit when it comes to learning. You could even choose to improve a skill that leads to a higher income down the road. Perfecting a new skill will remind you of your worth and capabilities beyond your relationship. Have fun with this one. The world is your oyster!

2. Go to the Gym

Make gym sessions part of your weekly routine and you'll see benefits beyond just your appearance. Not only will you look fitter and more toned, but most importantly, you'll *feel* stronger. And you'll instantly see a boost in your level of self-esteem and confidence. Working out is a great way to prove to yourself that you can overcome adversity – this determination and strength will extend beyond your time at the gym, improving your relationship and likely even your professional confidence. Take care of your body and your entire mindset will reflect this positive transformation.

3. See a Therapist

It's time to remove the stigma around therapy! You don't need a mental health condition in order to see a therapist. Having a session once a week or every couple of weeks is a great way to destress and declutter the mind. Getting restless emotions and thoughts out of the way gives you more time to focus on what really matters. Therapy can be especially beneficial for people in a codependent relationship. A neutral figure will be able to point out when codependent habits are surfacing and help you evolve out of them. They can help you tackle the root cause of your issues so you never again have to call yourself 'codependent.'

4. Experiment with Cooking Healthier Meals

We all know how to cook *something* in the kitchen, but how many delicious, truly healthy meals can you cook? In your spare time, why not experiment in the kitchen with some body-nourishing foods. When we focus our attention on feeding ourselves, our minds find a calm center. Why? Because we are going back to basics and doing something that literally keeps us alive. We are giving attention to the fundamentals of our being and this can be meditative. Try and cook with new ingredients, have fun with new flavors, and see what delicious creations you can come up with.

5. Plan Your Future and Set Goals

Now that you have some alone time, why not see if you can define your goals for the near and distant future? What would you like to accomplish? Where would you like to go? What are some habits you'd like to break and some better habits you'd like to pick up? While you're doing this, try and make your first draft of goals without considering what your partner (or anyone else) would say about them. Just focus on your goals and dreams. Once you clearly identify what these are, weight out how important each one is to you. How happy will you be if you achieve each one? Will the inability to achieve a certain goal lead to unhappiness? Answer these questions before thinking of what your partner would say. Consider making the goals that would make you deeply happy a non-negotiable.

6. Read a Good Book

They say the world's most successful entrepreneurs read dozens of books a year. It's no wonder why. Not only is reading entertaining, but it can broaden your horizons in ways that change your perspective and outlook for the better. Whether it's fiction or nonfiction, reading brings many benefits including memory improvement and stress reduction. Over time, you'll find your vocabulary expanding and it may even enhance your writing skills. Incorporate more reading time into your schedule (now that you have more peace and quiet!) and you'll supercharge that mind of yours in no time.

7. Start a Creative Project

You don't need to be an artistic genius to start a creative project. It's as simple as choosing a medium you enjoy and having fun with it. Encouraging your own creativity helps you destress and in the long run, improves your problem-solving abilities. Studies have even shown that creativity enhances one's ability to adapt to new changes. The next time you have time to yourself, why not try painting or sketching? Or pick up an instrument and learn to sing?

8. Learn to Develop a Growth Mindset

As you pursue new hobbies and skills in your spare time, try and develop a growth mindset. A fixed mindset is driven by the belief that everyone is born with certain talents and gifts, and all those who are not 'gifted' will never achieve the same level of brilliance. The growth mindset comes as a firm opposition to this, asserting that we can indeed reach the same level of brilliance if we persist and continue improving ourselves. While you have personal space, try to absorb this growth mindset into your mental space. Not only will this help you improve certain skills, it will also help you grow out of your codependency. You don't have to be codependent forever; a growth mindset will ensure you leave your old habits behind for good.

9. Take Breaks from Tech

While you're taking a break from your partner, why not take a Break with a capital B from all the chaos of the modern world? You can choose whatever timeframe you're most comfortable with – but it should pose a little bit of a challenge! For at least a couple of hours, turn off all your communication and entertainment devices. Completely disconnect from all digital distractions and do not communicate with your partner in any way during this time. Feel free to do whatever you like during this time as long as you are in charge of creating your own entertainment (do not go to a bar and watch their TV!) and you're allowing yourself to be alone with your thoughts. Practicing No Tech time can decrease anxiety over time as you begin to get used to silence and temporary disconnection.

10. Have a Conversation with a Stranger

This may seem like an odd suggestion, but learning to be comfortable around strangers has a number of different benefits. Not only do you improve your social skills, but you learn to become adaptable to different situations and different personalities. You also have no idea who you might meet! There are connections just waiting to be made all around you. Expanding your circle of friends is a great way to ensure you don't rely too heavily on your partner.

12 Self-Care Ideas to Make You Feel Like a Million Bucks

Of course, personal space should also be about self-care. When codependents are completely wrapped up in each other, they forget to take care of their own self. Often we don't realize how much we need self-care until we finally experience it. The result: we're calm, centered, and at peace in every single way. This puts is in a better mood, making us more pleasant individuals. In turn, this makes us better partners.

There's no need to reserve self-care for when we're completely alone. Self-care should be part of your routine and you can do it by yourself or with your partner close by. That's up to you. However you choose to care for yourself, make sure you always make time for it so it can be a consistent part of your life.

1. Bubble Baths

You've probably seen it happen in movies. During times of relaxation, a character is neck deep in a bubble bath surrounded by candles. Why not try it in real life? Bubbles or no bubbles, candles or bathroom lights, music or silence: the choice is yours. Discover what kind of environment helps you achieve a deep calm and try to get to that quiet place in your mind. Forget the world for a moment and relax.

2. Massage

Getting a massage requires no effort from you. Just find a spa or masseuse that you like the sound of, and enjoy being pampered. A massage session makes brilliant self-care because the kneading opens up the body and – of course – it just *feels* amazing. The gentle pressure all over the body relieves stress by releasing dopamine, reducing anxiety and instantly making you feel more calm, no matter what. It doesn't need to be complicated; just lay down and allow yourself to feel good.

3. Coffee and a Good Book

Since the dawn of hipster cafes, the coffee-and-a-book routine has become a brilliant modern way of achieving self-care. Get out of your space and spend a few hours in a coffee shop. Order a steaming cup of coffee or a creamy hot chocolate, find your spot, and finally delve into that great book you've heard so much about. Believe it or not, just getting out of your personal space can reduce anxiety. The coffee-and-a-book routine allows you to simplify your life for just a moment. All you have to do is enjoy your comfy spot, focus on your book, whilst nourishing your belly with warm, rich goodness.

4. Go Shopping

Let's preface this by saying: don't go overboard! Know what your budget and stick to it. And other than that? Have fun and treat yourself to whatever makes you feel good. There's a reason the term 'retail therapy' exists. When we shop, we get to indulge our wants and needs. This is good practice for the codependent who tends to be focused on other people's wants and needs. Take this moment to shut your codependent brain out and consider what purchase would excite you in the here and now.

5. Get a Makeover

Sometimes there's no better way to feel good than by making yourself *look* good. There are no rules to getting a makeover – just have fun experimenting with your appearance with the goal of making yourself feel attractive. If you're female, consider purchasing the services of a makeup artist. Both genders can enjoy getting a few different outfits for their wardrobe or freshening up with a new haircut. The possibilities are endless!

6. Talk to Friends

Talking and laughing with friends is its own form of therapy. While you're engaging in self-care, why not have a catch up session with some of your most trusted friends? Not only does this provide stress relief but it's been proven that spending time with friends leads to a longer lifetime and improved mental health. Whether you decide to indulge at a great restaurant or have a fun night in watching Netflix or a game, make sure that time with friends is a regular session in your schedule.

7. Write in a Journal

Journaling is great for codependent couples because it allows you to get in touch with your feelings. To keep the peace, codependents are known to shut their thoughts and feelings out – something that does not bode well for the health of the relationship. Journaling can help you declutter your mind and destress, allowing you to organize your thoughts and observe your inner world. Many people choose to write in their journals in the early morning or right before bedtime, as a way of calming the mind for the day or for restful sleep.

8. Meditate

When looking for the best self-care methods, meditation is suggested so often that it tends to elicit a roll of the eyes. There's a good reason why meditation is raved about; it has real, lasting benefits that genuinely make a difference to your mental well-being and life. To meditate successfully, one must try to clear their mind of all thoughts and simply be in the moment. To get started, try and focus your breath, and nothing else. Ideally, this should be done in a quiet space where one can sit down without being disturbed. Make meditation part of your self-care routine and you'll soon see reduced stress and anxiety, and an enhanced self-awareness and attention span.

9. Go For a Drive or Walk

This self-care method requires nothing but energy and time. Choose any starting point at all and just take a walk or drive from there onwards with no destination in sight. Just explore and keep going forwards. The purpose of this drive is to clear your mind and to have time alone with yourself, while still experiencing the motion of moving forwards. Going for a walk or drive is known to be emotionally healing; it allows you to be in full control of your path and destination, just going wherever you please and letting your thoughts find peace.

10. Redecorate

A fun way to achieve self-care is by redecorating your space. This could be anywhere you like. It could be your desk at work, your bedroom, or even your entire house. Redecorating can be incredibly fun as it allows us to use the creative side of our brain – but more than this, it is also an act of reclaiming our space and practicing our control over our surroundings. Make aesthetically pleasing choices and see if you can rearrange your belongings for the most convenience possible. Organize and decorate your space so that it becomes your own personal sanctuary. By the end, you should feel comfortable, relaxed, and inspired in your newly decorated space.

11. Exercise

Exercise isn't just a way to see more self-growth, it's also a great way to engage in self-care. It's only important that you don't overdo it and exhaust yourself. Whether it's a leisurely walk through the park or an intense session of pilates, exercise ensures that your body stays strong and capable. Many people think that exercise is so hard it can't possibly be self-care, but this is just a sign that you need it more than ever. Exercising allows us to reconnect with our vessel and to be more in tune with its needs and abilities. The rush of endorphins also means you'll instantly feel more positive about yourself and life in general.

12. Practice Gratitude

Believe it or not, it's been proven that practicing gratitude makes a person more happy. By training the brain to notice and be thankful for the positive things in life, we instantly begin to operate from a mindset of abundance. This improves our sense of self-esteem, our ability to empathize, and it even improves our quality of sleep. To begin practicing gratitude, find a place where you can begin making notes about what you're grateful for. This can be a special gratitude journal or it can be on the Notes app on your phone. Every day list down three things that you're grateful for in your life. Try and be as specific as possible. Remember that these don't have to be grand parts of your life, it can be as simple as the fantastic lunch you had or a great workout session. Just make sure whatever it is, you feel genuinely grateful for it.

Do not feel daunted by the idea of personal space. It's a chance for you to recalibrate, reenergize, and do what you need to do to sustain your own inner strength. It's a time to reconnect with the activities you enjoy and the purpose of your life. Learn not to see it as separation from your partner, but instead as powerful fuel for a healthy relationship.

Chapter 8: Healing Codependency For Good

A short message from the Author:

Hey! We've made it to the final chapter of the audiobook and I hope you've enjoyed it so far.

If you have not done so yet, I would be incredibly thankful if you could take just a minute to leave a quick review on Audible, even if it's just a sentence or two!

Many readers and listeners don't know how hard reviews actually are to come by, and how much they help an author.

To do so, just click the 3 dots in the top right corner of your screen inside of your Audible app and hit the "Rate and Review" button.

Then you'll be taken to the "rate and review" page where you can enter your star rating and then write a sentence or two.

It's that simple!

I look forward to reading your review as I personally read every single one.

I am very appreciative as your review truly makes a difference for me.

Now back to your scheduled programming.

We've broken down personalities of codependent partners, highlighted the habits that need to be eradicated, as well as the habits you need to start bringing into your life – but that's not all you need moving forward. The urges that lead to codependency run deep. Underneath the little habits and practices are some key and highly essential lessons. The smaller practices will certainly help in building a healthier day-to-day dynamic, but without absorbing these core lessons, you may find yourself relapsing back to square one. During particularly trying periods, feel free to return back to this chapter to remind yourself of what's important.

The Lessons that Break Codependency

- 'Tough Love' is Necessary – Embrace It

Don't shy away from the notion of tough love. Simply put, tough love is when we give our loved ones certain boundaries or constraints with the intention of helping them grow in the long run. Even if they don't realize it, tough love is for *their* benefit. To heal codependency for good, you need to start embracing practices of tough love. This means saying no and setting limits even when you feel sorry for them and want to say yes. Codependents may struggle with guilt at first so it's important that you make a mindset shift during these moments. Instead of focusing on their reaction in the current moment, think of the benefits they'll see down the road. Think of the life-altering lessons this will teach them and how life will reward them for it if they persist. Do not be swayed by the temporary discomfort and focus all your attention on the potential growth of the situation. Tough love is a different kind of loving behavior, but it is loving no less.

- Needs are Tools, not Enemies

In codependent relationships, the enabler tends to see their needs as obstacles. After all, how can they take care of their partners needs when their own are getting in the way? For enablers to continue breaking their codependent patterns, they need to stop seeing their needs as inconveniences. Our wants and needs are tools. They tell us about our state of mind and what we need in our life to find satisfaction. Our needs give us the direction we desire. It tells us what we need for growth and what you need to sustain yourself emotionally and psychologically. Needs are, indeed, tools and indicators of growth. Do not shun them away or the urges will only become stronger. We become unhappy when we ignore these urges and try to suppress them. A need signifies a lack and if left unchecked, this can lead to a kind of emotional or mental depletion. Your needs are akin to the red light that goes on when your car starts to need more gas. These lights do you a favor by letting you know when they need something to keep going as normal. Treat your needs the same way. Do not let those red lights start flashing!

- Nothing Changes if You Don't Change

By now you've probably been faced with some harsh truths about your behavior and relationship. It's profoundly important that you don't stop here. The knowledge that you need to change is not enough in itself to create change. You feel unsatisfied, unfulfilled, like your relationship could be much better, and you're right – now do something about it. Use feelings of dissatisfaction as fuel to start taking action. Your codependency will not heal if you don't begin working with your partner to find a healthier dynamic. If you find yourself reverting back to your old ways, expect to revert back to your old feelings of frustration. If you want better for your relationship, *be* better.

- Clinginess and Obsession are Not the Same as Love

When you're completely wrapped up in your partner, it can be easy to think this obsession is equivalent to love. There's a big misconception that giving until you have nothing left and merging your identity with your partner is what true love means, but this only results in codependency. Moving forward, try to shift your perspective on what love means. Remember that love isn't just about how you are as a single unit, it's also about how the relationship affects you as an individual. Does the relationship empower you to achieve your own dreams and goals? Or does it make you feel like giving up on the rest of your life? Does the relationship remind you of who you really are? Or does it completely eradicate your unique identity? Think of love in terms of the long-term future that you're building with your partner, not just about how instantly gratifying is. Try and understand that love doesn't take over our life; it helps the rest of our life to blossom. The more you cling to your partner, the less time and space there is for the rest of your life. Real love is about two whole people who come together in their full power, not two halves trying desperately to make a whole.

- Stop Feeling Defeated by Rejection

There's a reason why both partners fuel this cycle of codependency; they're afraid of what would happen if they stopped. The enabler is worried, on some level, about not being useful and the enabled partner is worried about being forgotten. Although both partners have different ways of coping, they're both trying to ensure they remain loved by the other partner. Why? Because the thought of losing their codependent partner is far too painful. Unfortunately, this type of mentality can backfire. When we are driven to act a certain way out of deep insecurity around loss and rejection, it can become a self-fulfilling prophecy. As difficult as it seems, both partners need to learn to be okay with the possibility of not being in their codependent relationship. In other words, they need to get comfortable with the idea of being single. When they think of losing their partner, it's normal to feel deep sadness but they shouldn't feel like their world will end.

Getting comfortable with the idea doesn't mean you want it to happen – it simply means that if it's right, you'll accept it. At the end of the day, rejection lets us know what's right for us and what isn't. Instead of trying to avoid rejection from your partner at all costs, learn to see it as a way to measure your compatibility. If you're rejected after trying your best, then it wasn't meant for you. One day you'll discover what *is* meant for you and you'll be fine.

What to Do If...?

You're trying to break a codependency and that's a big deal. Many scenarios will arise that leave you feeling confused and unsure of what the 'right' thing to do is for the health of your relationship. The next time you find yourself 'stuck,' turn back to this page. When you find yourself faced with any of these scenarios, this is what you should do:

- Your partner is not listening to your boundaries

By the time you finish this book, you'll likely feel motivated to strive for a healthier relationship. Unfortunately, you can't control how your partner feels. It's possible he or she isn't quite ready to make new changes. One of the ways they'll make this known is by refusing to abide by your newly set boundaries. If you make an agreement to split up chores, you may find that your partner still doesn't do their fair share, leaving you with most of the work.

Before you determine the best way to respond, answer these questions: how many times have you had to remind your partner of the boundaries? How many strikes have there been? How disrespected do you feel? Your intuition is a strong way to measure this situation. If you feel like your partner is trying their best but they're just struggling to let go of old habits, then be firm with them. Don't shy away from showing them you're angry or upset. Make it clear that this means a lot to you. If you feel disrespected and like your partner genuinely isn't trying, then reconsider your involvement in this relationship. You're trying your best and it's only fair your partner tries too. You're ready for a better relationship and as long as your partner is stuck in their old ways, they'll hold you back from growth too. You deserve better.

- Your partner is exaggerating their ailments as a way of rebelling against your new boundaries

You've tried to set boundaries with your partner and they've responded by exaggerating their condition. They are doing everything they can to make sure they appear more helpless. Hopefully, you know why by now. They want to keep the cycle going. They are likely afraid and nervous about the new turn your relationship is taking and they want you to start behaving like your old self.

Remember that your partner has been taught to equate enabling with love. This change of behavior is probably making them feel insecure, wondering how they'll continue getting love from you if you no longer feel the need to help them. Try and point out this behavior, gently. Draw what they are doing to their attention and explain why they are behaving this way. They may not even realize it and may be reacting purely out of insecurity. After this, continue to be firm with your boundaries but make an extra effort to show them love in ways that do not encourage codependence. If they enjoy receiving gifts, give them flowers or anything that encourages a new hobby – but all the while, do not back down on making them do their chores. Replace codependent behavior with other loving behavior.

- Your partner is suspicious of you whenever you have personal space

Since you and your partner are so used to spending a lot of time together, it can be jarring once you finally add personal space to your daily lives. As a way to cope, your partner may even become suspicious, believing that your behavior is caused by a more malicious ulterior motive. After all, they're used to seeing love as synonymous with time together. It will take time to adjust to this new perspective and it may result in resistance. They may even fire off a few accusations. For example, they may believe that the real reason you want space is to make time for cheating or because you're trying to break up with them in a kind way. These are some of the many accusations that enablers may hear.

See this behavior for what it is. Your partner has been taught that love means clinging to each other so naturally they think the reverse means you don't care about them. Obviously this isn't true, so take the time to gently reassure them. Remind them that the reason you're trying to change is because you want to ensure your relationship succeeds. Personal space is a way to make sure your relationship is healthy and secure, not desperate and clingy. Come up with ways you can reassure your partner without resorting to codependent behavior. Similar to the previous scenario, show them love in new ways, such as buying them a gift every now and then or writing them a heartfelt card.

- Your partner still can't take care of him or herself, even though you've given them space

As we've established, overhelping takes away autonomy and empowerment. To help your partner reconnect with their inner strength, you've likely given them space to learn how to take care of their own needs. This is a positive move, on your part. However, you may find that your partner is still unable to help themselves. They're trying but they're failing. They're incompetent, getting things wrong all the time, and overall, not doing as good of a job as you used to do.

In these moments, it'll be tempting to revert back to your old behavior. Watching them fail will make you want to help them again. If they're truly struggling, it's alright to give them a little bit of assistance, but other than this, try to stay firm. Otherwise, you may find yourself regressing. They're struggling because this is new to them. You've had your whole life to learn how to do it the right way, but they're only learning now. It will take some time. Expect it to take some time. Be gentle with them and do what you can to support them as they learn, but do not do the work for them. If your partner has trouble making their own food, buy them a new cookbook or pay for a cooking lesson or two – but do not give in and start making all their lunches for them again! Have patience and do what you can to foster growth.

- You've started to feel utterly useless and worthless

Until now, you've gotten by as the 'fixer' in your relationship. You got accustomed to helping your partner with every little thing and easing their pain whenever you could. But let's not forget, it's not just about what your partner receives from you; your satisfaction comes in the form of feeling needed. When you know you're helping your partner, you feel useful. You feel like you're doing something that matters. Breaking out of codependent habits means you're trying not to overhelp and this new change has caused you to feel a little useless. This may even result in some depression.

Remind yourself that you *are* helping by stepping back. By doing this, you're allowing your partner to learn their lessons and achieve self-growth. Understand that when you're not in a codependent relationship, helping and being useful manifests in different behavior. You're accustomed to the codependent way of 'helping' – which is actually enabling. When we *really* help someone, we do what's best for them. And in this case, *not* overhelping is what's best for your partner. Recognize that what you're really craving is the instant gratification that comes from enabling your partner. By not forcing them to do anything, you're allowing them to do what pleases them in the moment. This may look like it's good for them, but in reality, it is the furthest thing from helping. Remember this distinction and resist the urge to overhelp at all costs.

This journey won't always be easy. In fact, at times you'll struggle and feel like it's too difficult to handle. Of course it's hard – after all, you're breaking response patterns that have been hardwired into your brain. What's important is that you recognize the hardship for what it is. It's growth. Keep these core lessons at the center of all your decisions and you'll soon be able to proudly say, "No, I'm not codependent."

Conclusion

Congratulations on completing *No More Codependency*! By making it to this page, you've taken great strides towards a more sustainable and healthy relationship dynamic. This is wonderful news – not just for you, but also for your partner. You've proven that you are truly committed to a happier future with your significant other and that you're willing to do what it takes to quit your codependent ways. You are so much closer to success than you think! If you need more motivation, all you have to do is turn back to this book. Everything you need is right here.

Hopefully, this book has empowered you to keep making these big, powerful strides. It's important you remember that codependent relationships are not a life sentence; relationship coaches and psychologists everywhere agree that codependencies can, indeed, be healed with time. By adhering to the helpful rules and tips in this book, you'll soon see your relationship in a whole new light. You'll be a happier, more fulfilled individual and your relationship will blossom in turn. What's important is that you continue to persist and remain self-aware.

We've covered the in-depth details of codependency, identifying what it really means and what exactly makes it different to everyday dependence on our loved ones. It's important that you recognize this distinction as there's no need to eliminate all of your dependent behavior – some of it is perfectly normal. By now, you're well aware of the difference between the two. Codependent behavior doesn't mean never depending on our partner. It simply means having a healthy level of dependence and knowing who you are without your partner.

Before you move forward, it's essential that you figure out which codependent partner you are. Are you the enabler or the enabled? Try to approach this question without any denial. We've covered the likely backgrounds of each partner and it's possible you saw yourself in those descriptions. Perhaps you were even able to pinpoint the exact relationship in your childhood that gave you this codependent mindset. Now that you've finished this book, try and work through those memories. Which early relationship taught you to be codependent? Delve deeply into yourself and recognize that this early relationship was likely very dysfunctional. Treating your relationship the same way will only result in the same dysfunctions. You don't want that, do you? Of course not.

Once you commit to change, you'll need to start laying down some boundaries. This means saying 'no' and setting some rules where necessary. It means conveying to your partner, in some way, that you'll no longer be fixing every little thing that goes wrong. Doing this can be difficult, especially since you're not used to it. You may even have feelings of guilt or uncertainty around how to enforce them. Pay close attention to the tips we've covered and you'll soon see boundaries as completely natural. You'll suddenly find yourself with far more energy, now that you're no longer exhausted from over-exerting and doing more than your fair share.

Aside from this, it's also important that you and your partner work on building your sense of self. This may mean developing stronger self-esteem and self-awareness. Using the affirmations and exercises in this book, you can begin rewiring your psyche to produce more positive thoughts about yourself. How can you make the most of your gifts and positive qualities if you never realize they exist? Whether you realize it or not, self-esteem is a big part of healing codependency. You need to recognize that you are enough and that you are wonderful, even without a partner at your side. By creating a more positive inner dialogue, you'll help your relationship thrive.

After learning about boundaries and developing self-esteem, you were faced with some big challenges. Namely, destructive behavior. Hopefully, you were motivated and inspired to finally eliminate these harmful habits from your life. You can't evolve if you don't get rid of the obstacles. Once you've identified what these obstacles are, you can work hard on moving past them. Now that you understand the cycle of narcissistic abuse, you can hopefully recover from any abuse you've endured. If you're staying in a relationship with a narcissist, hold on tight. It may be a turbulent ride. Turn back to the section on narcissistic abuse and do your best to enact the changes that were listed – otherwise, you may find yourself stuck in a cycle that never ends. Remember this: if you don't change, nothing will!

With new detachment strategies and exercises under your belt, you can finally discover independence. Allow this to feel liberating because it is. Have fun with the challenges and enjoy how it feels to finally have personal space. By now, you'll know all about the importance of personal time and space. The next time you find yourself lost about what to do with yourself, rest assured you've got a solid list of ideas for what to do. Consider engaging in an activity that promotes self-growth or refreshes you through self-care. You need both in equal measure!

The core lessons that are integral to healing codependency have been summed up into bite-sized pieces. Turn back to the final chapter, if you ever find yourself wavering. Remind yourself of these lessons and make sure that every change you make is fueled by them. If a difficult scenario arises with your partner, this chapter will also give you ideas for what to do. There's always a solution as long as both partners are committed to growth. Don't let 'enabler' and 'enabled' define your life together. Explore your individuality, learn healthy detachment, and shower your entire life (not just your relationship) in love. Show yourself the same affection you're capable of giving someone else, and you'll move mountains.

Narcissistic Relationship

Discover How to Recover, Protect and Heal Yourself After a Toxic Abusive Relationship with a Narcissist

Table of Contents

Introduction **108**

Chapter 1 - Unraveling Narcissism **114**
    The 7 Warning Signs of Narcissistic Personality Disorder 114
    What Causes Narcissism? 120
    4 Types of Narcissists You Need to Stay Away From 122
    The 4 Types of People That Narcissists Are Attracted to 124

Chapter 2 - Staying One Step Ahead **127**
    11 Ways to Know You're in a Relationship with a Narcissist ... 127
    Dangerous Manipulation Tactics Used by Narcissists 134
    5 Things Every Narcissist Likes to Say 141
    5 Triggers for Narcissistic Rage 143

Chapter 3 - When Enough Is Enough **149**
    5 Essential Tips for Dealing with a Narcissist the Right Way 149
    5 Phrases to Instantly Disarm a Narcissist 154

Chapter 4 - Cutting the Cord **159**
    Why It's So Hard to Break up with a Narcissist 159
    The 7 Stages of Trauma Bonding 161
    How to Break Up With a Narcissist for Good 163
    Using the Gray Rock Method to Your Advantage 165

Chapter 5 - Healing From Narcissistic Abuse **168**
    The 5 Stages of Recovery from Narcissistic Abuse 169

5 Transformative Truths Every Victim Must Face 173
Essential Exercises to Strengthen the Healing Heart & Mind 178
Life-Altering Affirmations to Heal Past Hurts 180

Chapter 6 - Breaking the Cycle 185

6 Reasons Why You Keep Attracting Narcissists 185
7 Ways to Spot a Narcissist on the First Date 189
4 Ways to Stop Attracting Narcissists Once and for All 193
9 Powerful Tips for Developing Unbreakable Self-Love 196

Chapter 7 - Loving Again 201

7 Mistakes to Avoid When You Start Dating Again 201
5 Early Signs You've Finally Found a Good Partner 206
8 Great Habits to Start Your New Relationship the Right Way .. 209

Conclusion 214

Introduction

If you've picked up this book, you may be wondering if you're in a relationship with a narcissist. Alternatively, you may know you're in a relationship with a narcissist and are now wondering how to get out of it. Or you might be trying to assess if you really need to get out or if things will get better.

Our you may have come to this book because you have come out of a relationship that started off well but then left you so bruised and unsure of what went wrong that you are now looking for ways to heal and move on. You want to avoid a repeat of the devastation that a narcissist can wreak on your wellbeing.

Some of you may even be in a new relationship with someone who was hurt by a narcissist and wants to know how to help them move forward.

Whatever brought you here, you've come to the right place. In the chapters that follow, you'll learn how to identify narcissistic abuse and how to spot a narcissist, so you don't get stung again. You'll learn what they say, what they do, and how they react.

You'll learn how to protect yourself and use techniques to back away so that you don't attract the rage of this particularly difficult personality type. Most importantly, you'll be given the tools to help you recover from your experience and move on with your life to a happier future and better relationships.

As someone who has come across a few narcissists in my time, I have closely studied this troubling personality type and unlocked many of the secrets that make them who they are. Once you truly understand them, they lose their hold over you and reveal themselves for what they are — troubled and deeply lonely individuals who are sadly too damaged to enjoy healthy, balanced relationships with others. *You can't help them.*

Read this book, and you'll come away not only with greater understanding but also the tools to free yourself of the narcissist in your life. You can look forward to greater peace and security in your future relationships, a sense of safety and wellbeing, and greater self-confidence — something that a narcissist is quite skilled at undermining.

Here's what we'll cover:

- **How to spot a narcissist**

You'll find out what they'll say to you, how they will get under your skin and, most importantly, how they'll make you feel. We'll look at the different types of narcissists and some examples of how they tend to behave in certain situations, for example, on a first date.

We'll also look at what makes someone into a narcissist, and who they really are under that tough exterior (clue: very immature). Knowing just how small and frightened these people are beneath that smooth surface is key to understanding their behavior and to no longer being affected by it.

- **How to recover from narcissistic abuse**

A narcissist can do damage seemingly without regret. With their words and their behavior, they can have you doubting yourself, feeling unsure of your sanity, and living in a state of siege. They thrive on drama, discord, and conflict, while the people around them struggle to do anything apart from ward off their next attack. But you can break this cycle and not fall into it again.

In this book, you'll find out how to empower yourself, heal, and restore your sense of self-worth after narcissistic abuse. We'll also look at how to safely break up, disengage or move on from a narcissist without attracting their narcissistic rage.

- **How to deal with a narcissist in the moment**

Unfortunately, this personality trait is reasonably common. In fact, there are times when it's easier to simply get along with a narcissist. One example is when you have one at your workplace and you otherwise love your job. Another is when you have a narcissistic family member who you have to maintain some contact with for the sake of the wider peace. Why should you leave to escape just this one person?

The answer is, you don't. But what you do need are some simple techniques to prepare for those encounters. This way, you can deal with the narcissist in a calm, assertive manner "in the moment" when they attempt to push your buttons. The other benefit of this is that they are likely to get bored, move on to their next victim, and leave you alone.

- **How to escape from a narcissist**

One thing that narcissists cannot tolerate is being ignored or abandoned. This triggers all of their buried feelings, often buried from childhood, that led them to behave abusively in the first place. You can be certain that they will make leaving as difficult for you as it is for them. Once you have escaped, the narcissist in your life will simply move on to someone else — but before that happens, you can expect an escalation of all of their worst behaviors. In the most serious cases, you may be in actual danger.

However, there are ways to disarm the narcissist, back away slowly, and protect yourself. These can be learned. Most importantly, these techniques will make the process easier and less distressing for you. With some planning and easy-to-access tactics under your belt, you'll soon be looking forward to a more peaceful future, far away from this damaged and damaging individual.

- **How to help other victims of narcissistic abuse**

Dealing with a narcissist can leave you feeling isolated and unsure of your own sanity. Read on for essential tools that will help you not only recover yourself, but also spot the signs in other victims and help them to break free, too. As more is known of this personality type, I hope to see a world where they don't get away with it nearly as much as they seem to right now. Narcissists thrive on secrecy, and by writing this book and exposing their secrets, I hope you will learn from my work and come away feeling better equipped to simply disengage from them.

Through my writing, research, and close study of this particular personality type, I have helped many people escape from narcissistic abuse. Being caught in a relationship with a narcissist is something that I liken to the "frog in the pan of water" analogy — by the time the frog realizes the water is boiling, it's too late to jump out.

With a narcissist, you find yourself struggling to escape, worn out from their mind games, tantrums, and cutting insults. You end up doubting yourself. You may feel that you are enmeshed in a seemingly endless situation and no longer have the courage to escape.

Don't let that happen to you! Educate yourself, learn the signs to look for, and how to look after yourself and others. A narcissist has the power to cause great damage and untold hurt to those around them, but it doesn't have to be that way. They are only as strong as you allow them to be.

When you truly understand this personality type, you will see that they are not nearly as powerful as they appear. You will know exactly what to say and exactly how to behave so that they simply get bored and move on to someone else. In my experience, narcissists are very difficult, if not impossible, to treat.

They don't change, and they don't seek help. Often, they are perfectly content with the status quo and resistant to any change or greater equality in their relationships with others. Why would they want change when they have everyone dancing around them?

So, as hard as it is, there's no point wishing for them to change, either, despite what they may promise you at times. They will never change. All you can do is accept that and try to move on with your own life.

With my help, you can look forward to a happier future. You can escape. You can have a life free of drama and the toxic influence of a narcissist. You can feel greater contentment and a sense of safety and purpose. More importantly, you deserve to. Narcissists are very good at playing on our better selves, on manipulating the kindest and most empathetic people to meet their own selfish needs. You don't have to fall victim to this, and you don't have to get drawn into their games.

Read on to find out how.

Chapter 1 - Unraveling Narcissism

In this chapter, we start to unravel narcissism to find out what it is, what causes it, and how to spot it in others. We also look at the kinds of people that tend to fall prey to the wiles of a narcissist.

We'll give you some clues to look out for when meeting people for the first time, and odd behaviors to look out for. Let's go!

The 7 Warning Signs of Narcissistic Personality Disorder

Narcissism is a recognized personality disorder that is thought to affect around 6% of the population, though many who suffer from it may be undiagnosed. It's characterized by a grandiose sense of self (often very much undeserved), a ruthless need to exploit others, and a strong sense of entitlement. Narcissists are also prone to narcissistic rages. Unfortunately, they keep their true selves hidden and can also be extremely charming when they need to be.

Once you know what to look for, narcissists are generally easy to spot, and you can keep them at a distance without being drawn into their world. But what are you looking for?

Read on for the 7 key signs of Narcissistic Personality Disorder if you think someone you know or are close to may have it. See if any of it rings true for you.

1. They have a grandiose sense of self

The narcissist always has to be the best: the best looking, the most successful, the most interesting. While this can be charming or endearing in the short term, it quickly becomes wearing for those around this person, as they struggle to have their own achievements and needs recognized.

Narcissists believe that they are special and unique. They believe that they should only associate with other special people and that they deserve the best possible treatment and attention in any situation. They train others to believe this too, so that before you know it, you're dancing around this person and treating them with excessive care, often at a considerable cost to your own time, wellbeing, energy and personal growth.

They will also exaggerate and lie about their achievements, and downplay, ignore or refuse to acknowledge those of others. Whatever you may have achieved in your life, you can be certain that the narcissist has done it too — and done it better.

Classic narcissist behavior:

You: Oh, guess what? My novel is being published!

Them: That's nice. That reminds me, I'm going to write a novel. I love writing, and I was always very good at English. Everyone always told me I should write a book. Who is your agent, and can you send me their details? I would like to talk to them about my planned book.

2. They live in a fantasy world

In their own world, they are successful, wonderful, and there to be admired. If you support and reflect these beliefs back at them, you will enjoy their approval. If, however, you dare to challenge them on the truth or details of their many achievements, be prepared for a serious backlash. You'll soon learn to tread carefully around the narcissist to avoid any repercussions or **narcissistic rage**, which knows few boundaries.

Classic narcissist behavior
If a narcissist visits your home, expect to feed them, wait on them, and clean up after them, and possibly lend them money, without any reciprocation of the favor. If you visit them, expect to be given little to eat and to simply listen to them talk about themselves. After all, you are lucky to be around them.

3. They require lavish praise and undivided attention

If you're in the company of a narcissist, after a while you'll start to notice something: it's all one way. You are simply there to listen to them talk about how wonderful, talented, how special they are. They want you to hear how many friends they have and how successful they are in their career.

Try and get something back from them or ask them to recognize you in any way and prepare to be frustrated: the narcissist is simply unable to pay attention to anyone else. It goes against their belief that they are the one who must be looked after, deferred to, and fussed over. They find it incredibly difficult to focus on or recognize others.

Classic narcissist behavior

You are at a party, celebrating the pregnancy of a friend. The narcissist will use the opportunity to announce their own plans to have a baby and somehow you'll end up drinking champagne and congratulating them, while they stand in the middle of the circle, smiling and enjoying the attention. Meanwhile, the pregnant friend is forgotten.

4.   They have an extreme sense of entitlement

Of course, we all deserve to be treated with respect and kindness, but a narcissist takes this to another level. You may be groomed over time to accept their demands if you know them personally and accept that it's "just the way they are," but it's often jaw-dropping to see their sense of entitlement play out with other people.

Often, seeing a narcissist out in the world is a lightbulb moment for their victims. You may also see the most entitled behavior in how they treat others and feel embarrassed for them. You would be quite amazed at their ability to make the most outrageous demands, seemingly for the fun of it.

How do they treat waiters, reception staff, shopkeepers? They may be overly warm to those that treat them with deference, but watch out if someone dares to put them in their place or refuses to assist them with their often unreasonable demands.

Classic narcissist behavior

You're in a foreign city and looking for a bank. The narcissist will walk into a nearby hotel and demand that the receptionist looks up the directions of a bank, writes it down for them, and then — as an afterthought — gives them detailed instructions on various local museums. If the receptionist refuses to help them, they will feel extremely angry and become rude and petulant, and complain bitterly about how unreasonable the person was.

5. They exploit others without guilt or shame

We are all guilty at times of overstepping the mark with others, and for most people, once we realize this we apologize and make amends. We may feel shame or guilt and vow to learn from our mistake and do better next time.

But for the narcissist, there is no sense of guilt or shame. There is only rage and a sense of fierce injustice if they get called out for their behavior — after all, they are *special*. They are allowed to break the rules. Unlike normal people, the narcissist is constantly looking for a way in — and they are very good at playing on people's natural courtesy and generosity to meet their own needs.

Narcissists don't see any point in helping others for its own sake. All they care about is getting their own needs met, and they are prepared to behave as badly as they need to for this to happen. The only thing that may stop them is the worry that they are going to go too far and lose access to the person or thing they are exploiting: then, and only then, will they pull back temporarily so that they can continue to use and abuse in future.

Classic narcissist behavior

A narcissist will accept your offer to go out for the day, but will "forget" their wallet. You'll end up paying for their lunch, drinks, and entry fees. At the last moment, though, in a shop, they will suddenly "find" their wallet and buy themselves a new bag with all the money you've saved them. On the train home, they will mention that they'll pay you back, but you'll never see that money again, or even get a thank-you for treating them all day.

Or let's say you meet someone at a party who is a friend of a friend. They shower you with attention and through your friend, track down your email or phone number. Before you know it, they are passing through your town — because you had such a great chat at the party, is it OK if they stop by your house, around lunchtime? Before you know it, you're feeding them lunch and listening to them talk about themselves for two hours, lending them a book and helping them solve a problem with their phone — all on your day off.

6.   They bully, belittle, and humiliate

To control others, you need to keep them feeling small and weak, and no one is better at this than a narcissist. They are experts at hunting down your weak points or sensitivities and then using this knowledge to bully and humiliate you whenever you seem to be getting ahead of yourself. To them, it's all a game. They like making others feel small because it makes them feel powerful, and it suits them to do this to those close to them because it makes them easier to control.

Classic narcissist behavior

You're dressed up and feeling good about yourself, and the narcissist will make a snide comment about your appearance, laugh at you, or simply refuse to acknowledge the effort you've gone to. If you appear too confident, they will come out with a nasty comment about your hair or your clothes to take you down a peg.

7.   **They have no empathy**

This is perhaps the most chilling characteristic of a narcissist, as well as their central trait. They lack basic empathy and simply can not relate to the pain of others in any meaningful way. They may be able to fake it, but really, they feel nothing for the suffering of others. Some of the more malignant narcissists (more on this later) even seem to get some strange joy out of watching those around them suffer.

Classic narcissist behavior

You've just broken up with your boyfriend. You share the details with the narcissist and get no sympathy or comfort in return, just a bored comment about how the relationship was dragging on anyway and how you seem to always be so unlucky in love. They change the subject to talk about how well their own relationship is going.

What Causes Narcissism?

Narcissism is believed by many psychologists to have its roots in childhood. Often, it appears linked to a combination of both smothering a child with love and approval, and also neglecting them. Narcissists may have been sent to boarding school, for example, so they had holidays of luxury and privilege interspersed with long periods of institutional care where they felt alone and abandoned by their parents.

Small children tend to be quite selfish and lacking in empathy, as these are traits that diminish with maturity. The narcissist, however, never seems to learn to be kinder. They may have been overindulged as a child and allowed to get away with murder, yet also neglected by their main caregivers, never learning to feel empathy or think about the impact of their behavior on others.

Sometimes they have something happen to them that is so traumatic that they remain stuck in a selfish, immature way of dealing with others. Grown-up, but behaving like a baby. Again, this may be down to their caregivers not giving them the tools to treat others well.

As with all personality traits, it's impossible to say just how much can be put down to childhood experiences and how much is simply temperament and genes. What matters for those around the narcissist is how to deal with him or her, not what caused them to be the way they are.

It's important to remember, however, that the childhood roots of narcissism mean that it's very much a fundamental aspect of this person's nature, not something they can change, and not in any way your fault. You will find it very difficult, if not impossible, to change a narcissist. All you can do is change the way you react to them.

When is it narcissism and when is it just confidence or arrogance?

It's estimated that around 6% of the adult population suffers from narcissism. But what makes it different from the arrogance we see in popular culture? What distinguishes narcissism from the selfie culture and the self-promotion and showing off we see on social media, for example?

The difference often comes down to how authentic this confidence is — if it's genuine, it tends not to cause problems. But if it's hiding a much more uncertain person, it can be a disaster. While there is nothing wrong with demonstrating self-confidence in your life, even if it sometimes tips over into arrogance, narcissism is something different. They suffer from jealousy and are chronic "bucket dippers" — always seeking to dip into someone else's bucket of self-esteem in a flawed attempt to fill their own.

The narcissist is totally lacking in any form of self-confidence — deep down, they are actually a very small, frightened child. Their grandiose behavior is defensive and a way of protecting themselves from further harm. What looks like entitled behavior is actually an act, concealing someone with very little self-worth.

This is not true self-confidence, which is a trait that generally makes people more pleasant to be around. You can also be an arrogant person at times but still be a loving partner, for example. A narcissist, on the other hand, has a personality disorder and it's difficult, if not impossible, to have a healthy and mutually satisfying relationship with them.

4 Types of Narcissists You Need to Stay Away From

Narcissists come in different forms, and some are easier to spot than others. All, however, are worth avoiding. Here are four recognizable types and what to look for in each:

1. Overt narcissists

They make life (relatively) easy in that you can spot them a mile off. These are the kinds of people you find bragging on Twitter about their latest achievement or lying about how much their car cost, or how much they earn.

Overt narcissists are also prone to public blowups and meltdowns, which again makes them easy to look out for and avoid. They can be very charming and seductive when they want something, but once they have it, they will move on.

2. Covert or closet narcissists

These guys are harder to spot and better at concealing their true natures. They may present themselves as saint-like, doing lots of work for charity and high-profile good deeds. Scratch that pristine surface, though, or get them on their own, and you'll find a narcissist.

3. Toxic narcissists

Narcissism, like all personality traits, exists on a spectrum. A little is healthy, a bit more annoying, but a lot — dangerous.

Toxic narcissists are at the more extreme end of the spectrum, so be prepared for drama if you let one of these into your life. They may be spiteful, extremely nasty or bullying and generally make your life extremely difficult.

4. Psychopathic narcissists

I truly hope you never meet one of these characters. They are truly dangerous, showing no empathy or remorse, and actively seek to impose suffering on others. Murderers and dangerous abusers fall into this category. They enjoy the suffering of others and are vampire-like in their consumption of misery and pain.

The 4 Types of People That Narcissists Are Attracted to

One thing that you need to understand about narcissists is that they have very little sense of self. Instead of developing normal, healthy self-esteem, they ended up as adults feeling that they were both special yet very misunderstood — a strange combination, and not a happy one.

What they are drawn to, like vampires, is people with a good sense of self and a certain empathy towards others. A narcissist will want to both benefit from your kindness and also squash your self-esteem so that you give them more of your energy. They feed on the good feelings of others because they have none of their own to draw upon.

One of the terms you will hear in relation to narcissists is "supply." But what is it? Essentially, **narcissistic supply** is what they want from you — supply to them is attention, drama, focus, energy. You may have heard the phrase "she was sucking the life out of me." This is what being around a narcissist for any length of time feels like — you feel compelled to give them so much of yourself, while getting very little back, and you end up feeling exhausted.

Here are 4 of the features found in those who fall prey to the mind games of the narcissist. Keep in mind, though, that you don't have to give in to them. If you learn to spot a narcissist, you can put up good boundaries and protect yourself. In the following chapters, we'll show you how.

1. **Someone successful and talented**

Although you'll never get the narcissist to admit it, they may target you because they perceive you to be successful or talented in some way. Unable to deal with their feelings of jealousy, they will then make a game of bringing you down, humiliating you and destroying your confidence as a way of feeling better about themselves.

Does this actually work for them? No. But remember, the narcissist is very immature. They are like a four-year-old stamping on another child's sandcastle, which they wish they had built themselves. Taking someone else down may give them some temporary relief, but soon enough, those feelings of jealousy and inadequacy will return. If you're around when they do, prepare to be attacked once again. This is the cycle of narcissistic abuse, and you will soon come to recognize that the good days are always followed by bad ones.

Narcissists will also be drawn to successful people because they feel they can ride on your coattails and draw on your connections and talents to benefit themselves — for example, turning up at your professional events and using their connection with you to meet people and try to advance their own interests.

2. Someone who makes the narcissist feel OK about themselves

Again, you'll find that people who feel good about themselves tend to be willing to lend that same energy to others. So they'll give people compliments or reach out with kind gestures in the belief that this is just how you behave in life. Unfortunately for them, the narcissist will want more and more of these kindnesses, until the giver feels drained and exhausted by them. Narcissists are bottomless pits of need, and if you give them a hand, they'll take an arm.

Again, I can't emphasize enough how important it is to look not at someone's words — which can be very charming when necessary — but at how you feel around them. Do you feel on edge? Do you feel exhausted? If you are someone who tends to be kind and giving, be aware that sometimes, for your own sake, you need to hold back.

3.   Someone who makes them look good

It's not about you; it's about them. So if you have some talent, or are good looking, or impressive in some way, you may find a narcissist attaching themselves to you and feeding off your reflected glory. You may find the attention flattering, but after a while, you'll want to shake them off. That's when you realize it's not as straightforward as dealing with a normal person.

4.   Someone who indulges them and puts up with their behavior

Be careful of being too kind or understanding with a narcissist. While normal people won't take advantage of your kindness, you can be sure that this personality type will. They will essentially feed off your goodwill and attention, needing more and more of it. And if you attempt to back off or set some boundaries, be prepared for trouble.

So there you have it. With this chapter, we've looked at what makes someone a narcissist and what kinds of people they are drawn to. Read on to find out what to do if you have just realized you have a narcissist in your life!

Chapter 2 - Staying One Step Ahead

Narcissists are very skilled at manipulation, so it's all too easy to miss the early warning signs that you're in a dangerous situation with someone who seems perfectly normal and charming.

What you can arm yourself with, however, are some signs to look out for when you've just met someone and are wondering if it's "all in your head" or not. Narcissists are not quite as clever as they think they are, and you will soon learn to spot some common traits and signals.

In this chapter, we'll also look at some of the tactics used by narcissists to manipulate you, and some of the common phrases you are likely to hear from this personality type.

Finally, we'll look at narcissistic rage and its triggers. This is an important section to read as, if you haven't experienced it before, a narcissistic rage can come as a huge shock. You'll be left wondering what you've done wrong and how you can fix it.

11 Ways to Know You're in a Relationship with a Narcissist

1. They seem absolutely lovely at the start
You know what they say about something or someone that seems too good to be true. They usually are. If someone is so sweet, agreeable, and utterly delighted by everything you say and do, it should leave you

feeling a little... wary. No one is that nice, right? When is this going to turn?

Trust your instincts. This cannot be stressed enough. You may be falling prey to **love bombing**, which is just what it sounds like — being absolutely smothered in love and admiration.

Don't just look at what someone says or does. Look into their eyes — does their expression match their words? Narcissists can be incredibly sweet and charming, but they can't hide their cold eyes. So, if you feel like someone's words and expression aren't quite adding up, believe yourself.

Narcissists don't want the same things from a relationship that ordinary people want. While you or I may look for company, conversation, support and shared laughter, a narcissist is focused only on what they can get from you — be that attention, glory, time, energy, money and status.

They tend to see others only in terms of what they can do for the narcissist, not as someone to share a mutually supportive relationship. So when someone seems determined to win you over, to be bombarding you with texts and declarations of affection, take a step back. Enjoy the attention, certainly, but take it with a grain of salt. Time will tell.

2. They are incredibly selfish
This is a trait shared by all narcissists, and one that plays out in big ways and small. Notice what they're like to be around — are you the one doing all the listening, or do they listen back (and by that I mean,

active listening, reflecting what you say and genuinely seeming to engage with you as a person)?

Do you end up giving more — more money, more work, more emotional energy? When you come away from them, do you feel inspired and uplifted, or simply drained. A narcissist may be charming and funny, but they also have a way of taking up all the available oxygen in a room, of making everything about them. You may not notice this right away, particularly if you are someone who likes to give, but just start to notice and you may see a pattern of selfish behavior emerging.

Another point here: look at how they behave when no one is around. They may be good at the grand gestures when they have an audience, but how do they treat you when it's just the two of you?

3. They care more about the image of your relationship than the reality

Again, this is about the narcissist's obsession with appearances. Narcissists tend to be both secretive and obsessed with their public image. You may have been arguing with them that morning, but they will still post a loved-up picture of the two of you to their social media accounts and present a perfect image of your relationship to others.

With most people, life is shades of gray. But with this personality type, their need to be the best, the most popular, successful, and attractive trumps their need for any kind of authenticity. One of the things that come as a surprise to people in a relationship with a narcissist is that when they talk to others about how badly the relationship is going, they are often met with surprise.

"But she always speaks so highly of you!" is a common response. This is because narcissists want to give the impression of getting along with everyone and of sharing a wonderful intimacy with you to others. As well as wanting to preserve their image of themselves as a wonderful, popular person, this also means that others don't believe you when you say that the relationship is not as wonderful as it seems. So you end up feeling both isolated and confused — are you imagining things? (The answer is no.)

4. They are critical of everything you do

A narcissist likes to control others to feel more secure themselves, and one way of doing that is to criticize and find fault with everything that you do. The result is that you feel on edge, like you're walking on eggshells, toning yourself down to avoid further negative comments.

Be wary of those little comments about what you're wearing, your hair, your career choices, and small daily decisions — they may seem harmless on their own, but they can start to add up and chip away at your self-esteem, which makes the narcissist far more powerful than you.

If you're in a romantic partnership, look at how someone was at the start of your relationship — did they find everything you did wonderful? If that starts to change, you can doubt yourself. What are you doing wrong? How can you fix it, to get it back to how it was at the start.

Stop these thoughts! The problem isn't you.

5. You can't argue with them

With normal people, arguing may not be pleasant, but with a bit of give and take, you can either agree to disagree or move on to other topics.

Not so with a narcissist! They are simply unable to compromise or to acknowledge that they are wrong. Getting them to back down is even more challenging, and they never, ever apologize. Why would they? Doing that would be admitting they aren't perfect, and for the narcissist that is impossible to even contemplate.

6. If you disagree, you're the problem

Part of the narcissist's inability to ever admit they have crossed a line or done something wrong (which they frequently do) is that if you do disagree with them, you won't just be met with a flat refusal to acknowledge their mistake. Instead, you'll find yourself in the wrong and being attacked. Here's an example:

You: I really felt when we were out tonight that you were quite rude to me in front of my friends, and it made me feel bad.

The Narcissist: I don't know what you're talking about. That's not true. Why are you like this all the time — so angry and oversensitive?

See the difference? A normal person would listen, reflect on their behavior, and apologize. A narcissist will not only reject what you are saying; they will go further and make out that you're the one with emotional problems.

7. They don't have any close friends

A narcissist may have a lot of people around them who admire them, joke with them on social media and like their numerous selfies on Instagram. But do they have old school friends? People who have been in their life for a long time? Or is it all just superficial?

Narcissists tend to burn a lot of bridges, so if you meet someone and they appear to have no old friends at all, take note. It may be that they treat everyone so badly they are unable to maintain long relationships.

8. All their exes are crazy
As a general rule, if you hear this, run a mile. Often, the ex may well have been driven a bit crazy by the narcissist's behavior, but has since recovered and moved on. If someone seems obsessed with talking about their ex and his or her craziness, it's a big red alarm bell, and you should listen. Or you will be the next crazy one.

Also beware of the person who places all the blame on a failed relationship with the ex. Usually, a relationship fails because of shared problems or differences. It's rare for one person to be all bad and the other to be blameless. If this is how an ex is being presented, you may be in the presence of a narcissist.

9. They are suddenly nicer when you pull back
Narcissists are emotional vampires. They don't care about you as a person, but they do care, very much, about having access to your time, money, presence, and energy.

If someone treats you badly or suddenly shows their true self, it's natural to pull away. The other party may notice and apologize, perhaps, and you will both move on. With a narcissist, though, they are incapable of apology and reflection.

What they will do, though, is lure you back with kindness, extra attention, and charm. You'll know deep down that you're being played, but you'll also welcome the more reasonable behavior, feel relieved, and seek to move past it. And so the cycle will begin again.

10. They'll fight hard when you leave them
Relationships end, and it's sometimes a struggle to leave on good terms. But if a relationship has run its course, it can be done, particularly if both parties are committed to being kind and getting on with their own lives. Try and get away from a narcissist, however, and be prepared for a lot of resistance.

You may find yourself bombarded with phone calls, text messages, and even have them turning up at your door. They will also send in "flying monkeys" —people who believe the narcissist's version of events and will be convinced by the narcissist to call you up and elicit feelings of guilt and obligation to give the narcissist yet another chance. Even if they don't particularly want to be with you anymore, they will keep you dangling because they don't want to see you with anyone else.

Sometimes people decide that it's actually easier to just give in for the sake of a peaceful life — particularly if other people are being drawn into the drama — and so the cycle begins again. Once you have let them back, you can be certain that the cycle of indifference and nastiness will start again. Soon, you will probably find yourself being punished at some point for trying to break free at all.

11. You feel bad about yourself when you are around them

It's been said that you may forget what someone said to you, but you'll never forget how they made you feel. If someone makes you feel exhausted, drained, irritable, depressed, or insecure, take note. These are never good signs in a relationship.

A genuine narcissist can also make you feel frightened — in their body language and in the energy they are giving off. While their words may be conveying one thing, their physical presence and their eyes may be saying something quite different.

It's always worth listening to your gut in these situations and taking note of your bodily reactions as well as your more logical thoughts — they are equally important, and often your gut instinct is spot on.

If you notice yourself feeling anxious or on edge around someone, they may not be a narcissist, but you still need to acknowledge those feelings and set appropriate boundaries, even disengage gracefully. You don't need to have a huge showdown — sometimes, simply turning down the volume on a relationship is all you need to do to protect yourself.

Dangerous Manipulation Tactics Used by Narcissists

Narcissists have a number of tactics they use regularly to lure you into their world and keep you there. What is different from ordinary relationships is that there is always an element of control with a narcissist.

While in a typical relationship there is give and take, and a gradual building of intimacy and trust, with a narcissist it all unfolds in a way that leaves you emotionally vulnerable, weakened and at a real disadvantage. Look out for these tactics in your relationship and see if you notice anything familiar — if you do, you may well need to get yourself out of your current situation.

1.   Intermittent reinforcement

This is when someone treats you nicely, but only *sometimes*. You may put up with all kinds of shabby behavior — turning up late, showing little interest in your life, catty remarks and bullying — and then every so often, you are floored by how kind, loving, and understanding they can be.

This has a noticeable effect on your mental state. You'll feel quietly undermined by them, by their comments and behavior. You'll start to question your every move and walk on eggshells around them to avoid further criticism. You may even find yourself constantly thinking of ways to please them.

After a while, though, you might suddenly feel like you've had enough. Nothing you do seems to please them. You spend time with other people and realize how odd their behavior is in comparison. You start to wonder if perhaps you'd be better off creating some distance.

Bingo! At this point, **intermittent reinforcement** will kick in. You'll be suddenly floored by how understanding, receptive, and incredibly nice they are being. Just when you start to relax and think, *wow, they are really lovely*, the bad behavior will start again. This is a very clever tool, because people are naturally wired to go back for more when someone leaves them hanging.

Treat them mean, keep them keen, does, unfortunately, work for many of us. Another word for this tactic is **hoovering** — once they know they've gone too far, they'll start trying to hoover you back under their thumb with unexpected kindness and sweet-talking.

But this is no way to live and takes a huge emotional toll. If someone is nice to you, but only *sometimes*, take note. It's not healthy or normal behavior, and you deserve so much more. In genuine relationships, people treat each other well. If they don't, for some reason, they acknowledge it and apologize. If you find yourself being treated badly by those close to you, there's a big problem.

2. Gaslighting

This term *gaslighting* derives from the 1944 movie, *Gaslight*. In it, the abusive husband cleverly manipulates his wife into believing she is going crazy by changing her environment in all sorts of subtle ways. In her house, gaslights dim for no apparent reason, things go missing, pictures vanish from walls. She never quite knows if things are changing around her or if it's all in her head. Narcissists **gaslight** those around them regularly in all sorts of ways.

Gaslighters cause you to doubt your own sanity and keep you on unsteady ground by telling blatant lies that they then deny, making out that you are the crazy one. Some examples of gaslighting in a modern relationship might be:

Example one:

Your gaslighter tells you some unpleasant fact about yourself — for example, that you once slapped him across the face — and when you say, *no I never did that*, they say — *but you did!*

You wonder if you have simply forgotten it, or if you really did slap him across the face. You know that it's not in your nature to hit someone — yet he seems so confident that it's true. Who is right?

Example two:

Your gaslighter says he will take you out for lunch on the weekend. When you bring it up to arrange a time, he says, *no, I never agreed to that. I'm busy all weekend.*

You don't want to push it, because you know how upset he can get if he's challenged, but at the same time, you were looking forward to it. And surely, if he offered it, he would remember. Ultimately, it's easier just to let it go, but it leaves you feeling oddly mistreated.

Example three:

Gaslighting can also take place around boundaries. Let's say your friend asks if they can stay with you for a week. When after two weeks they show no signs of leaving and you push them for a definite end date, they fly into a rage about how unreasonable and unwelcoming you are being.

You wonder if you are being unreasonable. After all, they said they were only coming for a week, and now it's been two. Surely that's reasonable to ask? But they seem so angry, so maybe it is rude of you?

Maybe you are being selfish, as they say. No it's not, and no you're not. You are being gaslit.

It's important to note here that people can forget what they said or be vague for other perfectly harmless reasons. But watch out if you start to notice a pattern — what is being said seems to change constantly, or you don't remember saying or doing certain things that you are being accused of, or feel like you are being manipulated somehow.

Gaslighting is incredibly difficult to call out because it's the work of people who are setting out to deceive you deliberately, not the work of fair and reasonable human beings. Really, the best thing to do if you notice gaslighting is to leave — you will never win with someone who refuses to play fair.

3. Projection

Anything a narcissist doesn't like about themselves, they will project onto you and others. So while narcissists are some of the most selfish people you will ever meet, they are also the first to accuse others of being selfish. This may be people in their circle, or it may be politicians or public figures.

For example, a female narcissist may make frequent comments about "all men being a bit stupid," but is the first to cry sexism if a man doesn't shower them with admiration and undivided attention.

They will also accuse you of being a liar if you call them out on their own lies. You will never, ever hear an admission of guilt. All you will hear is a flat denial, followed up by a declaration that you are unfairly targetting them with *your* lies.

Narcissists are unable to reflect on their behavior and admit that they are in the wrong. Far easier to dump the blame and attending shame on you, and view themselves as the wounded party.

4. Nonsensical conversations

With most people, if you have an issue you'd like to discuss with them — perhaps to do with their treatment of you or your relationship — you would expect them to listen, reflect, and respond appropriately. Not so the narcissist! (Do you see a pattern yet?)

One of their most infuriating tactics is to shower you with **word salad** when you try and have a conversation with them about some aspect of their behavior that you are finding difficult. Prepare to be bombarded with bizarre observations, unrelated anecdotes, and strangely worded sentences that don't make much sense. You'll leave the conversation thinking — "What just happened?" while the narcissist goes on their merry way, knowing full well what they have done.

If you confront them, you'll be met with a flat denial. And, most likely, another generous serve of word salad. So really, there's no point getting into any kind of disagreement with a narcissist. It's like trying to argue with a toddler — you get nowhere.

Another thing to note here is that narcissists enjoy confrontation and argument. It fires them up to win and to leave you feeling like the bad guy. So the best thing to do is to avoid arguing with them at all — and further along, we'll learn some tactics for doing just this.

5. Vague or overt threats

Narcissists tend to be possessive and jealous, but they won't always come out and admit they are feeling this way. Instead, you'll receive a vague sense of unease if you do something they don't approve of — sulking, an angry tone, or a tantrum accompanied by threats.

Things that you would expect your friends to celebrate — a new job, some exciting personal news — will leave them feeling inadequate and abandoned. They don't like the success of others, as it draws attention away from them, so they will find all kinds of ways to burst your balloon.

If you feel you have to walk on eggshells around someone for fear of their anger, or if you stop doing things you'd ordinarily enjoy, such as going out with your friends because you're worried that you'll get in trouble, take note. This is not normal or fair behavior, and it reflects the narcissist's childish desire to have you always focused on them, and not on other things or people that make you happy.

Yes, it's a shame they react so badly, particularly if the narcissist is a family member, for example. But they won't change, so the best thing to do is to only share your good news with those you know will want to celebrate along with you. Ignore any threats and call out any sulking — you don't need to put up with it.

6. Baiting, shaming, insulting and name-calling

All of these tactics are used by narcissists, often in subtle ways that leave you wondering if you are oversensitive or just imagining things. Narcissists love to **bait**, which means saying something with the intention of hitting your weak spots or provoking anger. You take the bait, and suddenly you're being difficult and creating a drama out of nothing.

While most people, even if they know your weak spots (and we all have them) will take care to tread carefully around them, narcissists are the opposite. They will learn the things you feel sensitive about and take great pleasure in making you feel worse about them, all to make themselves feel more powerful.

Insulting and **shaming** are the same kinds of tactics — a narcissist will skilfully uncover your weak spots or things you feel self-conscious about, and then use this knowledge to insult and shame you later on. Often, this may be in the form of jokes, so that if you dare complain, you will be told you don't have a sense of humor, adding insult to injury.

5 Things Every Narcissist Likes to Say

Narcissists have a very predictable playbook, and because their tactics are so similiar, you will often here the same statements from them again and again.

1. **"That didn't happen." and "You're imagining it."**
These are both classic narcissists statements that underpin much of their gaslighting, as I described above. If you question something the narcissist has said or done in the past, perhaps in light of new information and because it contradicts what they are saying now, they will simply deny it. Denial is one of their first defenses because unlike normal people, they have no qualms about outright lying to save their own skin.

If you can prove without a doubt that they did do something, their final defense will be that you deserved it, often for spurious or unrelated reasons (remember that they also use **word salad**).

2. **"You're crazy."**
Because narcissists are unable to accept their ordinary flaws and vulnerabilities, be prepared to be told you're crazy if you dare question their version of events. They may not come right out and say this, but you might find yourself being reminded of that time you got very down, or they might refer in general terms to people who are crazy but in a way that makes you suspect they are referring to you in particular.

3. **"You're oversensitive."**
If a narcissist goes too far in what they say or how they treat you, don't ever expect them to apologize. They are, in their own eyes, incapable of being wrong, so an apology is beneath them.

What you will hear, however, is that you are overly sensitive. Or unreasonable. Or that you have always been a bit fragile. Or again, they will mention some other time when you showed emotional vulnerability, as a way of reminding you that you aren't as strong or capable as they are (although, of course, showing vulnerability isn't weak, it's normal human behavior).

4. **"It was just a joke! I'm *joking*."**
As well as being oversensitive, if you take offense at one of the narcissist's cruel barbs, be prepared to find out that you have "no sense of humor" or that you "can't take a joke."

Of course, you could retaliate by pointing out that what they said wasn't actually funny, it was just nasty, bullying or plain rude, but if you do, prepare for more defensive behavior.

5.   "In my experience..."

Or variations of the above, but essentially, if you talk about something that's happening in your life, perhaps a career success or anecdote, the narcissist will always be able to top it.

If you wrote a book, they wrote a bestseller. If you had a baby, they had five. This applies not just to achievements, but also drama. If you had your purse stolen, they stood up to a bank robber and saved someone's life. What is happening here is that the narcissist is unable to bear the attention being diverted from them — they want to be centered at all times, they want to be better, they want to be the hero in every story.

You may not realize this at first, so you talk a little about yourself as well as asking the right questions and listening. But you'll soon learn to keep quiet about your own achievements because if you speak up, you'll be put in your place with a ten-minute monologue about how they did it better. It becomes easier just to keep quiet and spare yourself the boredom of listening to their boasting (again.)

5 Triggers for Narcissistic Rage

So what is narcissistic rage? Think of it as the grown-up, much scarier version of a toddler temper tantrum. While most of us get angry from time to time, we are usually able to soothe ourselves, calm down, and take steps to handle our anger without lashing out at others or doing permanent damage to our relationships.

A narcissist's rage, however, is something else entirely. These personalities just loathe being told off or challenged. Being confronted or triggered about their shortcomings is not pleasant for anyone, but it's unbearable to them, and you will be met with such seething fury that you may feel physically assaulted. Ideally, according to the narcissist, you will learn your lesson and not do it again.

Or you will be met with icy silence and quiet passive-aggressive fuming. What you won't get is a clear explanation of what's going on or a way forward.

So what incites narcissistic rage? Essentially, anything that threatens their view of themselves as a perfect, successful, and extraordinarily special human being.

Here are some surefire ways to find out just how angry a narcissist can get:

1. **You confront them on their behavior**

If you call a narcissist out on their behavior, prepare to suffer. Even if you make your feelings known in a way that's constructive and diplomatic, you have broken the unspoken rule that the narcissist is never wrong.

Be prepared for flat out denial, rage, projection, and blame, but be assured that you will never see any form of acknowledgment that you have a point, and perhaps they could do things differently next time. If you really do have a point and they have no reasonable defense for their behavior, their final tactic is to collapse in a heap and cry, so you look (and feel) like the bad guy.

2. You ignore them

If you realize you are in a relationship with a narcissist and decide, for your own mental health, to back away or take some space from them, prepare to be challenged. Above all else, narcissists hate to be ignored, and if you set some reasonable boundaries around their access to you, expect them to be trampled on.

Often, this may be with someone, perhaps a family member or lackluster romantic partner, who typically shows little interest in your life, makes no effort to be around you, and makes unpleasant comments or criticism of your life choices.

But should you back off or start avoiding them, that will change. Expect to be bombarded with phone calls, emails and even unannounced visits to your home. This is because you are never allowed to call the shots with a narcissist, and you must always make them the center of attention.

And while they don't enjoy being around people in the normal sense, they also need you to give them **narcissistic supply**, which, as we have covered, is essentially your attention and energy. Should you try and take that away from them, they respond like addicts being deprived of what they need. Eventually, they will give up and move on to someone else. But before that happens, prepare yourself for a fight!

3. You laugh at them

One thing that narcissists value above all else is their public image as someone who is special, intelligent, and high status. While most people are capable of being self-deprecating or laughing at themselves from time to time, this is impossible for a narcissist. This is because it touches on their deep shame and hidden insecurity as someone who is ordinary, sometimes frightened, and not particularly special or talented. Laugh at them and prepare to be met with cold fury.

4. They don't get special treatment

Narcissists often have the people around them very well trained to treat them as if they are special and unique. But often, when they confront strangers, it doesn't go quite as they would like. They may demand special treatment from shop staff, or sit in first class when they have a third-class ticket.

When this happens, the unsuspecting stranger will soon find out just how 'special' the narcissist is and find themselves on the receiving end of verbal abuse or just more demands for attention that the narcissist actually needs or wants — they just want to make that person pay attention to them. They are the kinds of people to make rambling complaints to customer services departments, to badmouth companies with unfair reviews and to complain at length about poor customer service rather than shrugging their shoulders and taking their business elsewhere.

In personal relationships, you can also expect to see narcissistic rage if you pull back or refuse to pay special attention to the narcissist.

5. You take center stage

Let's say it's your birthday, and you want to celebrate with a meal or a birthday cake. While most people are happy to let the birthday girl or boy be the center of attention for one day, narcissists find this unbearable. Prepare for extra demands, sulking, an inexplicable tantrum or catty comments — because of course, it's all about them.

Another strange and noticeable feature of narcissists is that they are generally very bad gift-givers. Going out, choosing something that someone would love, wrapping it and presenting it to them is not something that narcissists see as worth doing. Of course, this alone doesn't mean that someone is a narcissist, but it's a common enough trait that it's worth mentioning.

What is the impact of the narcissist on you?

This is an interesting question, and one worth asking yourself. Surely, people can be difficult. Is it worth disrupting a marriage or romantic relationship or cutting regular contact with a parent because they are a narcissist? Is it not better, for the sake of peace, to simply put up with them? Breaking up families, leaving parents behind, leaving your boyfriend or girlfriend — these are all big decisions to make with life-changing consequences.

Is it better to just put up and shut up?

The answer is no. The narcissist will always have you believe that you should put up with them, that they didn't really mean it, that things will be different in the future. But they won't.

And every time you put up with it, every time you bite your tongue and attempt to get over feelings of hurt and disappointment for the sake of an easier life, you are doing two things:

You are affecting your future: your future happiness, your future goals, and aspirations, your children, and grandchildren. Every time you allow the narcissist to beat you down with nasty words and abuse, you are letting him or her rob you of a happier, more peaceful and productive life.

You are also affecting your own health and wellbeing in the moment. Of course, you just want the behavior to stop, for things to go back to normal. The easiest way to achieve that is to let the narcissist win. But play the long game. You can't see the impact of long-term, low-level stress and abuse on your mental health, but be certain it is having an impact. You have a choice to change things. And you deserve so much better.

Read on to find out how you can choose better for yourself.

Chapter 3 - When Enough Is Enough

So if you've read this far, you may have realized you have a narcissist in your life. The question for you now is, what are you going to do about it?

It may not be practical to break ties with them completely — perhaps you work with them, or they are a family member and the fall out will be too great if you cut them off completely — but what you need to do now is put your foot down. You need to change how you deal with them and prepare yourself for pushback. You need some strategies under your belt, and you need to believe in yourself enough to carry them out. Most of all, you need to heal, to practice self-care and to ensure that you set good boundaries so that you are safe from harm in the future.

You'll also learn about the Connection Contract and how this can help you get your own needs met. You may find, ultimately, that this is the first step in freeing yourself completely from a narcissist.

Read on to find out how to deal with a narcissist and protect yourself while they are still in your life.

5 Essential Tips for Dealing with a Narcissist the Right Way

Before we go much further, it's worth learning the five essential tips that you can keep in mind when dealing with narcissists. Remember, you are dealing with someone who does not have an ordinary personality. They don't follow the normal rules for human interaction, so you need to treat them differently, too. Most importantly, you need to protect yourself from harm as you set about breaking away. Here's how:

1.   Keep quiet and carry on

If you are working with a narcissist, for example, you may feel like you're the only one who noticed just how superficial their charm really is. It may even be tempting to confront them, or out them to others.

Don't. Bide your time, keep your guard up around them, don't share any secrets and remain pleasant and just a little distant. In time, the narcissist's mask with start to slip and they will reveal their true selves to others. At this point, you can watch from a safe distance. But you can't force this process without putting yourself in harm's way.

If you try and make this happen faster, you run the risk of inciting their narcissistic rage and having them turn on you, and you want to avoid that at all costs for your own wellbeing.

Remember, narcissists don't play fair, and they hate being confronted with their own shortcomings. It's a game you won't win unless you stoop to their level — and who wants to do that — so simply refuse to play. You'll be on your way to making your escape, and the longer the narcissist remains unaware of your plans, the smoother your exit will be. Keep quiet, build your escape plan, and work on your own wellbeing — which we will cover in future chapters.

2.   Disengage

Ultimately, what a narcissist wants is attention. Like a toddler, if they aren't getting positive attention, they will soon move onto behaving badly. If you consistently refuse to get drawn into their games, though, they will simply move on to someone else who is more willing to take the bait.

If you spot a narcissist, take things slowly and if you are proved right, be as boring as you can when talking to them. This is a great way to both protect yourself and hopefully see the back of them, too.

In some situations, you may not want to be boring. For example, in your professional life, you may want to shine and if your narcissist is in the same field, you may have to deal with some jealousy. Simply focus on doing your own work as best you can, never bite back, and be polite and professional at all times.

In personal relationships, start to step back a little, gradually. Stop taking the bait in arguments, stop expecting them to change, keep conversations light.

3. Work our your boundaries and make them clear

This is something you may need to do if you have realized you are in a relationship with a narcissist. These personalities constantly push boundaries in all kinds of ways — imposing on your time, your energy, your privacy and your personal life. Once you recognize this, however, you'll be in a stronger position to set and maintain boundaries around what is important to you.

For example, let's say a relative constantly makes negative or belittling comments about your career. Knowing this, have a few set phrases ready when the next comment comes: such as, "Hmm. I am really happy with how my work is going. It's not always a smooth road, but I feel like I'm making progress." Deliver them lightly, without any heat at all, and know that you have just made a choice to stand up for yourself that strengthens your position and weakens that of the narcissist.

And then change the subject, or put it back onto them and ask them about how their work is going.

Or perhaps the narcissist tries to draw you into a conversation about how your life is going, and you sense some probing. Be aware that narcissists like to learn your weak spots so they can reveal them to others or bait you with them at some later date.

In this case, again, remain friendly and neutral while giving nothing away that you don't want to — remember, just because someone has asked you a personal question it doesn't mean you have to answer it. Sometimes, simply replying with "What do you mean?" or "Why do you ask?" will put an end to their fishing.

4. Don't expect fair or reasonable behavior

Narcissists are chronic game players. But they also tend to have predictable methods of attack and will try the same thing again and again if they see it gets a rise out of you. Be unpredictable in response, and work on your own strategies, which might be as simple as refusal.

If they make a nasty comment, simply refuse to accept it. State mildly, "No. That's not true."

Never expect them to be fair or kind, and have your guard up ready to bounce back. Even a long pause followed by "What do you mean?" is effective and gives you time in the moment to stand up for yourself.

Leave them feeling slightly unsure about whether you're wise to them or not. They will never play fair, so don't feel like you have to be completely fair in response — play them at their own game, but innocently.

Another good tactic here, if you have to work with a narcissist, perhaps, or see one at a family gathering, is to prepare yourself in advance. Get a good night's sleep, eat well, get some exercise and learn some simple breathing techniques that will help you remain calm and cheerful in the moment. Narcissists tend to prey on the weak, so keeping yourself strong and healthy is a good way of fending them off. We'll look more at this later on.

5. Accept them

This is a hard thing to do, particularly if you are very attached to your narcissist — if, perhaps, they are your romantic partner, close friend, or parent. But if you can accept that they are a narcissist, that they cannot change and that you will never get anything different from them, your life will be easier. Part of the frustration of this personality type is that they can be so nice at times. You know they have it in them, so why can't they be like that all the time?

It doesn't matter. They can't. Often, they have no incentive to change. After all, the life of a narcissist is often superficially quite pleasant, especially with a few trained monkeys dancing around him or her. Yes, they have their demons, but they keep them well buried so mostly they are fairly content.

Accepting that your narcissist will not change is the first step in moving forward with your own life, free of their negative influence. You may not be able to shake them off entirely if they are a family member, but you will find they spend much less time under your skin than they are used to.

If you are in a romantic relationship with a narcissist, giving up on your expectations that they will change is the first step to freeing yourself, and moving on without them, or accepting them for who they are and finding other ways to get your needs met. You deserve better, after all.

5 Phrases to Instantly Disarm a Narcissist

1. "I agree." or "You're so right."

If you are in a work situation or family celebration, it's far easier to just go along with the narcissist. Agree with whatever they say, smile sweetly and be ever so slightly boring so that they quickly move on to someone else for more drama.

Challenging a narcissist is never really worth the energy as you will end up feeling attacked and unworthy if you do so — they cannot tolerate it, and if you try, you will soon realize just how difficult it is for them. What's more, they will seek to win the argument at any cost, and you will end up feeling attacked. Far better to smile sweetly and move on to other things — such as doing something that will make you feel good.

2.   "What will people think?"

One thing the narcissist values about all else is their image. If you want them to do something for you or just behave themselves, be sure to remind them that their behavior will be visible to others.

One of way doing this is inviting other people into a situation. Let's say you're arguing with them. Say, "Look, I think I'll have a chat to so-and-so about this and see what they think" or, "Should we get Dad into the room too so we can talk about this together." They will quickly change their tune if they realize you are prepared to make others aware of their behavior and not keep it quiet.

3.   "I'm sorry you feel that way."

This is a great way to defuse an argument with a narcissist. It puts their feelings firmly back onto them and is neutral enough to discourage further attacks. You aren't apologizing or taking the blame, but you are acknowledging that it is hard for them to be challenged.

4.   "I can live with your faulty perception of me"

Again, this is putting the narcissist's feelings and opinions back onto them. Let's say you have set a clear boundary with a narcissist that they aren't happy with. Now, they are attacking you and saying that you're being difficult and awkward and that you should give in to them.

Instead of saying, "No I'm not!" and getting into a defensive mode, stating calmly that you can accept their faulty opinion does two things: It tells them that they are wrong, but you aren't going to bother trying to correct them. Instead, you are going to accept that *they* are wrong, and move on. It leaves them with nowhere to go because you aren't taking on their negative attitude towards you.

Essentially, you are saying that you have no interest in controlling their thoughts, even though you don't agree with them or accept them in any way — which is a healthy attitude to take towards anyone, really.

5.   **"Your anger is not my responsibility."**

Again, you are putting their behavior back on to them. This one may make them absolutely furious — narcissists tend to hate any form of self-help talk or what they see as new-age nonsense. Just repeat this back to them, more than once if necessary, and get away from them if you can. They will soon get bored and move on.

How to Protect Yourself from a Narcissist

Protecting yourself from a narcissist isn't easy, but there are a few tactics you can try. If you aren't yet ready to leave a relationship with a narcissist, you may want to consider forming a **connection contract** with them to get what you want from the relationship.

What's a connection contract?

Put simply, a connection contract is a written agreement setting out your baseline for how you wish to be treated. Should the narcissist break this contract, they no longer have the right to enjoy a connection with you. If you are in a relationship with a narcissist, it may read something like this:

"I don't want to listen to putdowns or be yelled at or criticized unfairly. If you are incapable of doing this, I will leave."

For a narcissistic parent who wishes to visit you, it might be more like this:

"You can stay at my house for three nights, but while you are here you are to engage positively with my children, and not yell or scream to me or anyone else who lives here. Nor do I want to give you money — you need to handle your own finances and pay for your own expenses at all times. If you can't agree to these conditions, you will need to pay for a hotel and we can meet for coffee."

Essentially, a connection contract creates a crystal-clear and neutral set of guidelines about what will be tolerated and what won't. If the narcissist breaches this, you don't need to get angry or argue, you simply point out that they have broken the contract and therefore they are no longer welcome in your presence.

Yes, it's tough and it's blunt, but it takes the pressure off you to constantly be wondering what is acceptable and what isn't. With a connection contract, everyone knows what the rules are, and if the narcissist breaks them (and chances are, they will), you can point to the contract and keep your cool.

When is it appropriate to use a connection contract?

A connection contract may come in handy when you have already had several blowups and confrontations with a narcissist, and they know that you are not happy with their behavior but they are unwilling to change or acknowledge that they have done anything wrong.

Essentially, it takes over from the arguing and sets out what you don't see as acceptable. They might read it and want to argue again, in which case you can simply say that you don't want to argue further, you just want to go with what's written down.

It's a final way of trying to get a narcissist to behave themselves, and while it may not be successful, it does at least show that you mean business.

Chapter 4 - Cutting the Cord

Why It's So Hard to Break up with a Narcissist

Let's say you've read this far and realized you are in a relationship that is toxic to your own wellbeing, and you need to get out. This may be someone you have been in a romantic relationship with, or it may be a family member or close friend you need to back away from. Whatever the situation, you need to follow some trusted strategies to protect yourself while you go through with this process.

One thing you need to bear in mind as you make plans is that getting out of a relationship with a narcissist is **not like breaking up with most people**. They don't like it, and they will make it extremely hard for you.

If you have fallen for a narcissist, you will be enmeshed in what psychologists refer to as a trauma bond. As humans, we are wired to feel close to others. So the narcissist's tactic of love bombing at the start of a relationship, or when we start to pull back, will naturally make you feel closer to them.

But eventually, a narcissist will slowly but surely turn on you. You will feel confused and insecure because you never quite know where you stand. This uncertainty makes you less confident and easier to manipulate — all tactics that the narcissist will employ without conscience to gain the upper hand in the relationship. You will feel confused because you had bonded to them in one of their nicer moments and now you are seeing a different side to them.

You may know the relationship is bad for you and that this person makes you unhappy or fearful, but somehow you have lost the courage to look after yourself and leave. You're also doubting yourself — after all, you seemed to make them so happy at first? Surely for things to change, you must have done something wrong, and if you could just work out what it was, you will get things back to how they were? And every so often they are utterly lovely, which keeps you hanging on.

Narcissists are also very good at isolating their victims, so you may feel like you have no one to turn to. This isn't true. Chances are, there are old friends or family who will embrace you if you tell them the truth about your relationship with this person. They may already be aware of the problems and are waiting for you to speak up. The fact is, relationships shouldn't be this hard.

So how did you get into this state? Well, you're human. It happens. Some of us are more vulnerable than others to the charms of the narcissist, and that is something you may need to think about in future — we will look at red flags for future relationships at the end of the book. But essentially, narcissists are very good at what they do, and at creating a trauma bond.

Trauma bonding works a little differently depending on whether it's a long-term relationship — such as with a parent — or a new, romantic partner.

With long-term relationships, it's more of a constant cycle between loving behavior and abuse that can go on for years and is established in childhood.

With romantic relationships, it tends to be that things start off well and deteriorate. Either you get out at the first sign of trouble, or you get caught into an abusive cycle that can go on for years — if you let it.

The 7 Stages of Trauma Bonding

1.   Love bombing
You are perfect and you can do no wrong, and you are won over by their charm and attention. They are flattering, kind, affectionate and seem completely in love with you. Of course, being human, you enjoy this. But of course, with the narcissist, it will never last.

2.   Trust
You believe everything they are saying, and start to trust and believe in them. While there may be some small part of you that knows it is all a bit too good to be true, they also draw you in with small acts of kindness and intimacy that make you believe and trust them. You've simply never met someone this wonderful before, and they seem to feel the same way!

3.   Criticism begins
The love bombing tails off, slowly or sometimes very abruptly, and the nitpicking and criticism start to escalate. Suddenly you are not quite so perfect. This stage may be accompanied by increasing demands on your time and energy, conflict and a feeling of despair or

confusion, as you wonder what has changed, and how you can get back on firmer ground again.

4. Gaslighting
This new state of affairs is your fault. If you just did things differently, or you weren't so crazy or irrational, it would all be just fine. You start to doubt yourself, partly because they seem so convincing. They have done nothing wrong. It's all in your head.

5. Control
You go along with what they want because you start to believe that you are in the wrong and this is the only way to get back in their good books.

6. Resignation and increased despair:
Things seem to be getting worse. If you try and fight back, you are met with more abuse. You feel lonely, sad and isolated.

7. You're addicted
You know this person is bad for you, but somehow you keep going back for more, and all you want is to win back their approval and see their kind side. With a parent, this is because we are naturally wired to love our parents, no matter how inadequate they are for the job.

With romantic relationships, it's often because we have a vision for the relationship and its future in our head, and we know it's going to be painful and lonely to give it up and go back to searching again. Far easier to stick it out and hope for things to change. You're also weakened by their constant low-level abuse and not feeling strong enough to get out.

How to Break Up With a Narcissist for Good

Breaking up with a narcissist is not an easy process, but it is worth it. Mainly because the relationship is never going to give you what you need, despite the occasional good day. You are looking for something that just isn't there. Leaving this person behind will free up space and energy in your life for better things, healthier relationships and increased happiness. You are allowed to do that — in fact, I am giving you permission right now! But how do you do it? Read on to find out.

1.   Prepare yourself
Get as much information about narcissists as you can. Study this book and other resources, and know that you are doing the right thing for your own wellbeing.

2.   Distance yourself gradually
Be a little less available and a little more boring. Let them think that they are getting bored of you, even, and see if you can slowly disengage rather than letting them realize what you're doing — which can incite narcissistic rage.

3.   Reconnect with others.
This is a great way of breaking the narcissist's hold on you. Find ways of letting others back into your life, no matter how low and isolated you might be feeling. Call up an old friend, go to something that interests you, join a club. Whatever it is, break out of your isolation and surround yourself with healthy people and you'll start to feel better.

4.   Think of an excuse

Try not to make the breakup or distancing about them. Talk about what's better for both of you, and find ways of making it seem more like their idea than yours. Don't fire them up, accuse or tell them their faults — this is unbearable to them and will only make leaving harder.

5.   **Make a clean break**

Don't drag it out — once you've decided to leave, go quickly. Once you've left, don't contact them again. Stay strong and don't be tempted back by love bombing, which will come. Often, with a family member, it's impossible to make a clean break without a huge amount of disruption within the wider circle of family members. In this case, it's often easier to simply move away or go low contact, which is when you keep contact to a minimum and protect yourself with firm boundaries.

Many children of narcissists will state that the best thing they did was put physical distance between them and their narcissistic parent. It broke the strong emotional hold and also allowed them to really feel safe and happy in a place with no reminders of childhood pain.

6.   **Expect and plan for some retaliation**

You'll get people calling you, worried about you — those **flying monkeys** that the narcissist is so good at calling in. You'll get someone else trying to build a bridge. You'll receive phone calls, unexpected visits, letters with insincere apologies in your mailbox. Prepare for all of this and remain strong.

Eventually, if you remain neutral and firm for long enough, the narcissist will get bored and move on to someone else. But it will take time. While that's all going on, put in place some habits to protect you — get lots of sleep, exercise and good food to help you remain calm and focused in the face of the narcissist's outrage. We will cover this later on.

7. **Be kind to yourself**

A relationship with a narcissist can leave you feeling quite drained. You can expect some feelings of grief and a sense of loss, and even failure. These are all normal feelings and they will pass. Give yourself time and space, get some counseling if you need it, and take it easy.

Keeping a journal where you go to unload your feelings and also remind yourself of why you are doing what you are will keep you focused. When the narcissist starts love bombing, read back on your journal to remind yourself of just how nasty they are capable of being, no matter how delightful they are being right now. They won't and can't change, so getting away is the right thing to do. Remind yourself of this when you start to wobble.

Using the Gray Rock Method to Your Advantage

Above all else, narcissists love drama. They are also very competitive and envious, so if you have anything exciting going on in your life they will seek to feed off it — and try and steal away your joy in it. Narcissists love to blow out the candles on someone else's cake.

So how do you deal with this? Don't put the cake in front of them. The Gray Rock Method is a wonderful tool for dealing with narcissists. It goes against our normal instincts, but that's what you need to do when dealing with this personality type.

So how does it work?

Picture a gray rock. No color, no life, nothing to see here. And then, quite simply, behave like one. It's as simple as that. This trick is essentially making yourself appear so dull, so boring, that the narcissist has nothing to feed on and will soon (hopefully) move on to someone else.

What narcissists want is your energy. If you are feeling good, they want to take that from you. If you have some exciting news, they want to top it. If you have something painful going on in your life, they want to get up close and see your pain. They are the true definition of emotional vampires.

Give them nothing but a boring gray rock.

When they come back to you, looking for shiny treasures to steal, continue to give them nothing. Respond to their requests for information with boring small talk. Never tell them what's going well in your life, because they'll find a way to ruin it for you. If they probe, just tell them it's all been pretty quiet. No news.

Gray Rock is a good way of getting yourself written out of the ongoing melodrama that is the narcissist's life. They'll need to go looking elsewhere for their fix, and you'll be free to enjoy a more peaceful existence.

This is hard to do. There's always going to be a part of you that wants to win them over — particularly if they are a parent. After all, aren't they supposed to be happy for their children? Isn't that normal?

Yes, it is normal. The thing you have to remember, though, is that you don't have to be a good person to become a parent. In fact, you can be a thoroughly unpleasant person and have lots of children. It's a sad fact of life that the most undeserving people can be blessed with children, but they are emotionally unequipped to love and care for them.

Thankfully, this isn't the case for most of us. But if you drew the short straw, you are better off accepting it and looking for love and approval elsewhere than trying to get it from someone who doesn't have it in them, even if they are your mother or father.

With a romantic partner, you may find yourself wanting to impress them, to win them over and get things back to how they were at the start. Sadly, you can't. Their initial charm was an act, and what you are seeing now is their true self. Stop trying to win them over, and put your energy and time into building a happier future, far away from this damaged soul.

A note for your future self.
Chances are, you won't get into another relationship with a narcissist in a hurry. You have learned your lesson, and you'll know to pull away the minute you see signs of love bombing or sudden nastiness (more on this later.)

But here's a powerful quote from writer Maya Angelou to keep you safe:

"When someone shows you who they are, believe them the first time."

Chapter 5 - Healing From Narcissistic Abuse

If you are reading this book, chances are you are feeling bruised and attacked as a result of the interactions you've had with the narcissist in your life.

Psychologists now recognize that emotional abuse — the kind that you cannot see and leaves its bruises on the soul, not the body — is just as damage and traumatizing as physical abuse. Those who have experienced it often say they would rather be hit physically because wounds to the psyche are far more painful and debilitating.

It's also now recognized that psychological abuse can lead to the same kinds of trauma that result from single traumatic events, such as a burglary or mugging. Because the narcissist's abuse takes place over a long period of time, it can be hard to see the wounds and damage you have sustained. Instead, victims have a feeling of having been attacked or wounded that will take an equally long time to heal from.

Survivors of single incidents like car accidents know this instinctively, and while the damage can be deep, you can recover. The difference with narcissistic abuse, however, is that you may on some level feel it was your fault. The narcissist is very good at making you doubt yourself, at planting little seeds of uncertainty, all the while painting themselves as blameless. It's no wonder you feel like you're under siege or suffering from deep trauma when you encounter a narcissist.

In this, the most important chapter of the book, we will turn our attention from the narcissist and back to where it should be — on you.

We will look at the stages of recovery from narcissistic abuse, and how each one will play out.

We will also reveal the transformative truths that every victim must face up to if they are to recover from their experience. Plus, we will provide you will some essential exercises to strengthen and heal your mind and heart.

Finally, we will offer you life-altering affirmations to heal past hurts and to repeat to yourself like a mantra as you begin the exciting process of moving on from this toxic relationship and starting the next, happier chapter of your life.

The 5 Stages of Recovery from Narcissistic Abuse

Recovering from narcissistic abuse is similar to recovering from the death of a loved one. Particularly if you have loved and believed in this person for a long time and been taken in with their stories, it is hard to accept that they aren't who they said they are in. In fact, they aren't even close to how they portray themselves.

Recovery can be broken down into five stages. To some extent, your healing process will depend on your personality and the narcissist in your life. It's also important to note that there may not be a moment when you say you are completely over what has happened. Abuse leaves scars, and even if they heal over and no new ones are formed, they are still there. But they will make you stronger and more compassionate, so don't feel like you are changed for the worse, or irreversibly damaged. You have simply changed and grown up a little more, as we all do (apart from narcissists!)

Here is a rough guide that will help you understand the recovery process better.

Stage 1: Emergency mode

Let's say you've had what you expect to be your final showdown with the narcissist. You've told them it's over, you've left the building or put down the phone, and you are determined that you won't let them back again.

You might be getting messages from them or have them turning up at your door. Or you might be hearing from them through other concerned bystanders, sent in by the narcissist to play on your guilt, fear, obligation, and sympathy.

What you need right now is emotional safety. Talk to someone who understands the narcissist and won't place any blame on you. Tell yourself you are doing the right thing. And most importantly, do nothing to punish yourself. No bingeing on food, no ruminating or self-blame, no alcohol or drugs.

Practice **radical self-care**: treat yourself as you would a loved one who has suffered an injury. Here are some suggestions:

- Provide yourself with rest, good food, warm baths and even a bunch of flowers. Shop for and cook your favorite comfort food.
- Get some fresh air and gentle exercise.
- Listen to uplifting guided meditations on YouTube.
- Keep busy, put your house in order with some decluttering.
- Go for a swim or whatever exercise makes you feel good.

- Read a book or watch a funny movie.
- Make some plans for the future — a journey, a project, a new area of study.
- Get back in touch with nature: a walk in the forest or by the beach, or just a trip to your local park. Whatever it takes!

You can see from this list that it's about getting back to basics: doing the kinds of things that make a small child feel good. Keep it uncomplicated and know that you are doing the right thing by looking after yourself.

Switch your phone off if you need to and stay away from social media, where you may find your abuser trying to track you down. At this stage, you may be traumatized from the abusive contact and it's crucial to focus on calming yourself.

Stage 2: Moving forward and getting angry

Here, you'll start to feel your energy returning and you may have moments of rage and anger as you realize just how much time and energy the narcissist stole from you.

You might also feel angry at yourself — for letting the narcissist get away with their behavior for so long, for not speaking out or standing up for yourself. This is all totally normal and just means that you are moving forward and growing, not that you have failed or done anything wrong.

You may slip back into stage one, especially if you have contact with the narcissist. It's important at this stage to acknowledge your anger but not get stuck in it. Spending too much time online talking to other sufferers, for example, may not be the best idea as it can keep you from moving forward in your life.

If you find it really hard to move on, or you feel like you are going round in circles, this is a good time to see your GP and talk about getting some professional counseling, if you think it might help.

Stage Three: Should you get back in touch?

Now comes the point when you have forgotten some of the details of what went on, and more importantly, the unpleasant feelings may have faded. You start to remember the narcissist's good points. You begin to think that maybe it wasn't as bad as you remember, and maybe you were simply overreacting or being too sensitive.

Perhaps you want some closure, or a chance to see if they have mended their ways (they haven't.) Perhaps you simply miss the good times. You might also start to hear from the narcissist around now, as they begin to miss your attention and think of ways to lure you back in.

Remain strong. Don't go back — there is nothing there for you but pain. Letting the narcissist back into your world may send you straight back to stage one, or worse, you may find yourself back in a relationship with them, and the cycle begins again.

Stage Four: Achieving distance

This is the point at which you have had some time to heal and surround yourself with normalcy. You have moved past a lot of the fiercest emotions and you are starting to get a clearer understanding of what happened to you and why you were drawn into the relationship, or how you found your way out of it.

You may still have bad days, though, when you blame yourself or find yourself believing what the narcissist said about you.

Accept those feelings, sit with them, and they will pass. You are getting closer to being healed and moving forward with your life. The narcissist was wrong about you, and you did the best you could at the time.

Stage Five: Accepting and moving forward

You continue to move forward. You have a good understanding of your own strengths and weaknesses. Now, you are increasingly able to reject the things that the narcissist said to you.

Perhaps you have had some therapy and you are thinking about how to form healthier relationships in the future. You have formed some good daily habits to help you feel strong and safe (more on this later) and you are planning a happier life for yourself.

Above all, you are free of the narcissist and the toxic influence they held over your life.

5 Transformative Truths Every Victim Must Face

1.   The narcissist will never change in the way you need them to

Obviously, everyone is capable of change and personal growth. We all develop in all kinds of ways, some of us more than others. But the narcissist is very resistant to change, and you should never waste your time and energy hoping that things will be different.

For a start, it leaves you stuck in a position of waiting. And people can stay in that place for years. You may have moments when you see the possibility of things being different — for example, the narcissist has behaved badly, you have shut them out, and they are now luring you back in with promises that this time things will be different.

They won't. All that will happen, if you let that person get close again, is that the cycle will begin one more time. And then again and again. Even if they were to change, perhaps after many years of therapy, they will still be lacking in basic empathy. And do you really want to spend years of your one precious life waiting for someone to be better? All that time, all that energy, could be far more productively spent on other endeavors and more deserving people.

2. They aren't a different person with others and it wasn't you that was the problem.

Don't believe you are the only one to struggle with this person, although they may make you feel that way. Yes, it may seem like all is well in their other relationships, and you were the one that caused problems. But they aren't different towards other people. They are the same person with everyone.

The only difference is that you are seeing the outside of those other relationships, not the inside. Narcissists are incapable of treating anyone with kindness and decency. But they are also both secretive and obsessed with image, so chances are, their other relationships are also lacking and toxic, but they just hide it well.

3. They abused you deliberately and it wasn't "all in your head"

Because narcissists are so good at what they do, and at keeping their tricks just below the radar, you may start to wonder if you are imagining things. You might wonder if they are genuinely nasty and abusive, or if they somehow don't quite realize that what they are saying and doing is hurtful.

Yes. They know exactly what they are doing. There is no excuse for their behavior, although you will probably hear a few excuses: they are getting older (elderly narcissists are very good at hamming up their age when it suits them), or perhaps they had an unhappy childhood and you should actually feel sorry for them.

No. Sorry. Not good enough. Plenty of people have miserable childhoods and don't go around making others feel bad. There is no excuse for abusive behavior. This pity party is something that narcissists are very good at throwing when it suits them, particularly to target empathic individuals who will feel sorry for them and forgive them their behavior — only for it all to start up again one more time.

What compassionate people find hard to understand about narcissists is just how much pleasure they get from manipulating, exploiting and playing with others. Most of us don't enjoy those things and find it hard to imagine feeling happiness at the suffering of others. But narcissists do. They feed off the drama, the misery, and it gives them a sense of power, control and meaning in their otherwise empty lives. Sadly, there is no getting away from this, no higher self you can appeal to in the soul of a narcissist.

Nor is their abusive behavior accidental. A good question to ask yourself, if you are wondering about something a narcissist said or did, is — who was with you when they said that? Were you alone? Or did they say it in front of others? Anyone who can change how they behave depending on who is listening knows exactly what they are doing.

And even if they are unwell, it's not your problem. You have the right to protect yourself and live a life free of narcissistic abuse.

4. Recovering will take time and isn't a process you can rush

Unlike a single traumatic event, such as a car crash, narcissistic abuse takes place over a long period of time. While physical wounds can heal, damage to your mental health takes longer.

What this means is that you don't have to forgive your abuser or sweep your feelings under the rug.

If you feel sad or angry about how you were treated, that isn't a sign of weakness. It's a reasonable response to what has happened to you. Nor do you need to forgive or feel compassion for your abuser. After all, they feel no compassion for you.

The narcissist wants you to doubt yourself, to minimize what happened and to believe that you are exaggerating or making it out to be worse than it was. This isn't true. Narcissists are truly dangerous and disruptive people, and you can take as long as you need to in healing from your experience.

5. **All emotions are valid**

There is no right way to feel. You may have felt, with your abuser, that certain feelings or reactions were unacceptable. Narcissistic parents are very good at training their children to subdue emotional responses and never complain, for example.

But all of your emotions are valid, and you have the right to feel them and express them appropriately, whatever they are. You have the right to feel **angry** for what has been said and done, as long as you aren't expressing your anger in a way that is destructive to others.

The trick is to use your anger productively: Use it to drive you forward, to energize you and to put your feelings into things that will further your own life. It can be a creative force for the good if you channel it and use it wisely!

You also have the right to feel **grief**. This isn't a weakness, it's an acknowledgment that you have lost someone you cared about, or at least the idea of who they were to you. Feel your grief, honour it, and move forward.

It can be helpful to take some distance from your emotions, to see them as separate to you: perhaps visualize your emotions as clouds that move through the sky. In the same way, they move through your body and simply pass. You don't need to fall apart: simply feel them, acknowledge what you are feeling, and let it sit with you for as long as you need to.

If you want to shift an unhelpful emotion, here are two things you can try.

- Bodywork: We hold emotions both good and bad in our body — just think of how differently we look, move and sound when we are feeling happy and when we are sad. So it makes sense, then, that bodywork is a way of shifting emotion. This might be through massage with a skilled therapist, yoga, meditation or a long walk. Swimming and being close to the water is also very healing for our emotions.

- Talking to a therapist skilled in post-traumatic stress disorder is also helpful as you work through emotions, and they will have specific techniques you can use to move forward.

Essential Exercises to Strengthen the Healing Heart & Mind

As you begin your healing journey, you may find journaling your thoughts and feelings useful. This can be a brain dump style of journaling, where you simply get all of your thoughts and memories out of your head and onto your page, or it can be a guided series of questions to help you ask yourself how you got into your relationship with the narcissist and what you have learned.

Read on for some simple writing exercises that will clarify your inner thoughts and feelings and make moving forward a little easier by asking you some questions about your experience.

Find a time when you won't be interrupted and you are feeling strong, curious and ready to move forward in a significant way to get the most out of this exercise. Take as long as you need to, and feel free to return to these questions and your answers when you feel uncertain or upset. You will find your answers and your own inner wisdom very powerful. Ready? Let's go!

1. What are your false beliefs about the relationship?

Here, you can note down anything you believed about the person and your relationship with them that you now feel is false. Here are some ideas about things that you may have believed:

- Did you feel the problems were all your fault? None of us are perfect, but everything can't have been your fault. Start to unpick this and see if you gain a clearer picture of your relationship.
- Did you feel there were things you could have done to change the relationship?
- Did you feel he or she treated others better, or in fact does he or she treat everyone with a degree of contempt?
- Do you feel you will never find someone else? Is this true? Do you have other people in your life who care for you?

2. Is there anyone in your childhood who encouraged you to take on the blame?

- Sometimes, with a narcissist, we find ourselves taking on the blame for everything that has gone wrong, while the other person gets away looking like the innocent party.
- Is this a pattern from your childhood? Does it feel familiar to you? Is it true, or, like most children, were you just doing the best you could and making a few mistakes along the way?

3. What do you get out of protecting your abuser and taking the blame?

Perhaps you have some idealistic picture of how your relationship with this significant person should be, and you want to hold on to it. Perhaps you fear that if you stand up for youself you'll end up alone.

What is holding you back from facing up to the truth and leaving this person behind?

4. What are some alternative viewpoints you could come up with?

Finally, look at all the beliefs you have written down in part one, and come up with some alternatives that are realistic and feel true to you. For example, if you felt like it was all your fault, write down the ways in which you tried to make things better. Then list down the things that definitely weren't your fault and were simply the narcissist behaving badly.

Use this writing to return to when you are wavering or overcome with self-blame for what has unfolded. Taking the time to reflect on what has happened and challenging the status quo and the story your narcissist has told you is a way of replacing unhealthy beliefs with ones that are kinder and will help you move forward.

Life-Altering Affirmations to Heal Past Hurts

Add to your journal some affirmations that resonate with you, and use these to strengthen you when you are feeling overwhelmed. Again, this is something for your own private use and you can use it however you like, in ways that feel helpful and appropriate to you.

1.   "I am healing."

This is perhaps the most powerful affirmation and one that you can use to counter any negative thought spirals when they come up. Healing is a long, slow process, but it can and does happen.

Healing may not be a straightforward or linear process, and there will be setbacks along the way. But you will heal.

2.   "The past is behind me, and I am focusing on the present and the future."

It's easy, particularly when you are having a bad day, to get stuck in the past: regrets, rumination, thoughts about what you could have done differently or reliving horrible moments with the narcissist. Forgive yourself when this happens, and commit to the present and the future.

When you do get stuck in the past, the above affirmation can keep you steady. There is nothing any of us can do to change the past. All we can do is acknowledge what happened and use what it taught us to drive us into a happier future. It's also a good reminder to value the present moment.

3.   "There is absolutely nothing wrong with this moment."

Again, the past can rear up to haunt us at vulnerable moments. When that happens, focus on the present. Stand outside, listen to the birds, feel the sun on your face and remind yourself that you are safe and free from harm.

4. "I am a loveable person who deserves to be treated with respect and kindness."

This is the belief that narcissists are so very good at trying to dismantle. They are incapable of offering others love, respect, and kindness, or of feeling these things within themselves, so they do their best to make you feel like you don't deserve them, either.

Once you get away from a narcissist, you will need to work hardest at this affirmation. It means exactly what it says, and it is true!

5. "I deserve self-care."

This one is a life-long affirmation. We talked a little about self-care earlier in this chapter, and it is something that will really help you on your healing journey. It's also a way of putting yourself first — not all the time, of course, you're not a narcissist — but enough that you feel looked after and loved.

This isn't a selfish act; it's actually a way of ensuring you can take good care of others too. You can't fill up the tanks of others, such as your children and friends, when your own tank is running on empty. So look after yourself.

6. "I know what I know, and I trust myself."

Narcissists are experts at gaslighting and manipulating, making you doubt your own reality so they feel more powerful.

This affirmation seeks to counter that by putting you in charge of your own head and encouraging you to trust and believe your own intuition, thoughts, and feelings.

7. "I have the right to boundaries."

Protecting your boundaries is another act of self-care that you will need to work on as you recover from narcissistic abuse. It's particularly important as you can expect that the narcissist may lay low for a while, but will always return at some point to have another go at you.

Remain strong and unyielding, and quietly protect your boundaries at all times.

8. "They don't miss me; they miss the power."

If you feel sad for the narcissist because they seem lonely or try and get back in touch with you, remind yourself of who they really are with this affirmation. They never really loved you. It's not because of anything you did wrong, but because they simply aren't capable of love. What they do miss is having the power to mistreat you.

9. "My success is my response."

When anger strikes — and it will — don't lash out at them. This is exactly what they want you to do, as if you are showing emotion it means they still have power over you. Instead, repeat the above affirmation and use its energy to do something positive in your new life: work goals, a creative project, an exercise goal, or some self-care.

Work on things in your own life and let your happiness and future success be your revenge. Karma has a way of unfolding in its own sweet time — so you don't need to give it a push. You're too busy with other things.

10.   "I have good friends and family around me."

As well as repeating this to yourself, seek out those who make you feel good and who you love and trust. Being around a narcissist is like being in a cold, dark room. Look for those people who make you feel like you're standing in a warm pool of sunlight, who treat you with kindness and warmth. Good friends and loving family members are the best antidotes to a narcissist you will ever meet. These can also include work colleagues, neighbors and the new people who appear unexpectedly when you make room for them — all those people in your life who treat you with respect and kindness. Treasure them, enjoy them and keep faith that they are out there.

Chapter 6 - Breaking the Cycle

In this chapter, we want to talk about how you can avoid narcissists in the future. We will look at why you might attract the attention of narcissists and how you can spot a narcissist

Finally, we'll get creative and provide you with some methods for developing self-love and self-care, along with various practices to cultivate inner peace and happiness. These techniques will not only make you feel good, they will also provide you with protection against any narcissists in your life. Let's get started.

6 Reasons Why You Keep Attracting Narcissists

First of all, I need to clarify the above statement. It's estimated that around 6% of the population suffers from Narcissistic Personality Disorder. So if you are out and about a lot, working, going out and meeting people in your daily life, chances are you will come across a narcissist or two.

The trouble isn't encountering them or even attracting them. Because they burn through relationships more than most people, they also tend to hone in on anyone new, seeking fresh attention. The problem is letting them hang around. Narcissists are very good at spotting those who are going to put up with them, and who are therefore ripe to be exploited. So it's not about attracting narcissists — we all do at times — it's about letting them in your door.

Here are some questions to ask yourself about why you may have accepted a narcissist into your life that will help you both understand yourself better and be more aware in future about what to look for at the start of a relationship.

1.   Do you tend to put up with other people's selfishness?

Some of us are more tolerant than others, and if you suffer from low self-esteem or were raised in an environment where you were expected to accommodate selfish behavior, such as that of a parent, you may be conditioned to put up with selfishness. Narcissists will very quickly work out who will put up with their games and who won't and will hone in on those who tend to be more accepting and easy-going.

You don't need to be too wary or suspicious — after all, most people aren't narcissists. But don't feel you have to let everyone in straight away. Taking the time to get to know people slowly is a better strategy and if you do notice someone seems a little selfish — dominating in conversation, letting you pay for everything — take note and slow down in what you give them.

2.   Do you have boundaries around what you will and won't tolerate from others?

This can apply to friends, family and romantic partners equally. If you are someone who tends to feel taken advantage of, you may also be a target for narcissists. Look first at your own treatment of others — are you respectful of others, do you ensure you treat everyone as you would like to be treated yourself? Once you know you respect other's boundaries, why not insist that your boundaries are also protected?

This means thinking about how you would like others to treat you, and speaking up when you aren't happy about something. It's something you can learn to do, so if you feel like this may be one of the things that the narcissist saw in you, look into ways of strengthening your boundaries — we will cover some here, but a few sessions with a therapist is a great starting point.

3. Do you tend to stay for longer than you should in a bad relationship?

Backing out of a relationship that started off well but has since gone downhill is not always easy to do. At what point do you end it? How do you go about it? Should you stay, just to see if it improves?

If you are someone who finds it hard to know when to finish something, when to let go and move on, you may sadly be someone that narcissists are drawn to. If you feel that a relationship hasn't turned out as you would like, and you are unsure about whether you should leave or stay, there are a few things you can do.

First of all, remember that relationships are always changing. They get better or worse, but they never stay the same. The trick is to look at the pattern — if the relationship started off well but has steadily worsened, and you are feeling bad about yourself, then it's time to step away. It's simply not worth your precious time and energy to stay in a relationship that isn't making you happy. Never.

4. Are you someone who puts up with being devalued?

A narcissist will always start out lovely and charming, but let them in, and you'll start to see their true self. This may start with a subtle put-down or slightly off comment. Or you may realize that they never have their wallet during dates. Overall, they seem to always take more than they give in terms of time, energy, and effort.

If you are someone who has a tendency to put up and shut up, you are the ideal target for a narcissist. This doesn't mean that you have to get into a shouting match with them when they behave badly, it just means that you need to watch out for this tendency to be too much of a people-pleaser. Ensure that the people you bestow your time and kindness upon truly deserve it, and give it back, too.

5.   Do you tend to excuse other people's bad behavior?

It's good to give people the benefit of the doubt. Everyone has bad days and no one is perfect. But if someone's behavior is consistently difficult and you find you are always trying to find an excuse for it, this is a big warning sign.

6.   If someone is abusive, do you leave immediately?

This, more than anything, is a huge red flag. We all have different levels of what we will tolerate, depending on how we were raised and our own temperament and personality. If someone grew up with a parent who was violent, for example, they might have been groomed to see this behavior as acceptable or simply what happens in relationships.

If you feel you are someone who puts up with more than you should, get curious about this. Talk to a therapist or do some reading about what constitutes emotional abuse as well as physical abuse. Learn more about listening to your gut instinct and the warning signs of abuse. All of these things can be learned and will protect you from harm in the future.

7 Ways to Spot a Narcissist on the First Date

As we now know, narcissists are good at charming others, at seeming incredibly caring and understanding — until you get to know them. Then, it's a different story. But how do you filter them out before you get hurt? It's not easy, feeling a connection with someone makes it even harder. Fortunately, there are some warning signs.

1.   They have planned out the date out in detail

People who can't plan anything can be frustrating and at first sight, someone who seems to be in control of every detail of a first date may be a welcome change.

But pay attention to those early interactions — do they let you choose the venue, or do they insist on deciding? When you get there, do they say "Would you like me to order?" or do you make that decision together?

Someone who seems to want to be in control of every detail may be simply organized, or they might have a controlling and narcissistic personality. It's too early to tell either way — but just be curious, and take note.

2.   Love bombing

We've already looked at this in detail, but it's worth mentioning again as it's such a typical narcissistic trait, and one that can easily win you over if you aren't clued into it. If your date agrees with absolutely everything you say, something is up. No one is that nice or that agreeable. While it's flattering to have someone so seemingly in tune with you, if you start to feel like you're being played, you probably are.

Also look out for dates who start making too many plans, too quickly. On a first date, you should feel like you have a little time to breathe and reflect afterward, not find yourself lining up another meeting straight away.

Narcissists are very good at charming people and then before you know it they are in your life, settling in and taking over your time, your energy and your money. Be cautious. If something seems too good to be true, it usually is.

3. Lots of subtle bragging

It's an interesting fact that those who genuinely have the most to brag out — wealth, success, talent, beauty — tend not to brag at all. Instead, they seek to make others feel good because they have no need to seek approval from others themselves.

The out-and-out braggers are easy to spot and almost comical in their efforts to boast and impress with their money, power and success. But watch out, too, for the humblebraggers and the stealthy boasts that gradually add up to a picture of someone who feels that they're superior to everyone else. These are the really skilled narcissists, and if you noticed a few too many brags, you may be in the company of one.

4. **They are rude to staff**

How someone treats wait staff and others who are there to serve is always telling. Do they demand, complain and act superior, or do they make jokes on their behalf or try to humiliate them? Do they insist on sitting in a particular spot, or have some kind of problem with the restaurant's environment? If you see someone doing these things, it's a big warning sign that they may soon treat you the same way.

Being rude or getting angry over everyday annoyances like slow service in a restaurant is also a sign that they may have problems with anger management. Sure, everyone has bad days and gets annoyed, but if someone seems to have no sense of perspective and can't keep their cool in public, you may have a problem.

And also look out for anything weird around money — as we have discovered, narcissists tend to be bad gift-givers and are often stingy with money. Red flags here include suddenly disappearing to the restroom when it's time to pay the bill, refusing to leave a tip, or forgetting their wallet.

5. **What they say they want and their history don't add up**

If someone acts like they are desperate to settle down, marry and have children, be cautious. No one should be talking long-term on a first date (or second, third, or fourth...) Dig a little deeper and ask about someone's recent romantic history. Do they have a series of short-term relationships and dramatic breakups behind them? Do they have ex-partners that they still talk about a lot? All of these points may mean that you are in the company of a narcissist who tends to churn and burn through romantic partners.

6. They get you to reveal your insecurities but guard their own

Narcissists are very good at probing and digging around to find your weaknesses and the things you feel a little sensitive about. In time, they will use these to make themselves feel more superior and to needle you when they want to put you in your place.

Yet, you will never see them admitting their own insecurities in any meaningful way. While you spill your secrets, they will simply listen, smile and perhaps say something cutting to twist the knife a little.

If you come away from a date feeling like you've been way too candid and vulnerable, it may be a sign that you've just met a narcissist. Meeting new people should make you feel good, uplifted, encouraged — it shouldn't make you feel small or exposed.

7. It's all about them

The best conversations are a two-way street — some listening, some talking, some shared laughs, and observations. But not so with the narcissist, who isn't there to learn, listen and enjoy, but to be admired and fawned over. If someone talks non-stop, and you find yourself needing to disappear to the restroom just to get a break from their incessant chatter, be warned — this is your future.

If every anecdote you tell seems to segue into a similar story about something they did, but better, it's yet another warning bell. Narcissists find it very hard to listen. Usually, they seem distracted, they fiddle with their phone or don't quite meet your eye. They prefer to be discussing their own skills and talents than learning more about the people around them. If it's all about them, prepare yourself for the possibility that you may be in the company of a narcissist.

Another thing you might notice is that they talk very flatteringly of other people they know — friends, work colleagues, family members. You feel yourself getting ever-smaller in comparison to these wonderful people, and wonder why you are spending a date hearing about how special someone else was — shouldn't there be some focus on you? (Answer: yes.)

What to do if you realize all this on the first date?

Don't panic. Enjoy the evening for what it is (a learning experience!) and be sure to debrief with a trusted friend afterward. Spotting a narcissist early and setting up your boundaries accordingly is a useful life skill and one that is worth knowing!

4 Ways to Stop Attracting Narcissists Once and for All

If you feel like you keep attracting this type of person into your life, you are probably desperate to halt the pattern. After all, why would anyone want to invite such difficult people into their lives?

The truth is, the narcissist is there to teach you something. And until you learn it, they will keep coming back. See them as a teaching tool and they are suddenly so much easier to deal with. But what are they there to teach?

Essentially, it's people-pleasers that seem to attract narcissists. Docile, easy-going types are their favored prey. If this is you, there are ways you can change this dynamic.

1.   Don't make so many excuses for people

If someone behaves badly, they are in the wrong. Full stop. It doesn't matter how hard their childhood was, how stressful their job is — there is no excuse for abusive behavior. Don't excuse it. Don't empathize. You aren't their doctor and you aren't their punching bag. It's not your problem and you can't fix anyone but yourself.

Yes, it's hard to walk away from people. It's hard to accept that you can't fix someone, even if you care for them. It's hard when you know how forgiving you are, how kind and how good the relationship would be, if only they weren't so nasty. But you need to put yourself and your own physical and emotional safety first.

If someone is abusive towards you, walk away. It truly is the key to a happy and safe life, and you deserve it.

2.   Spot the red flags and trust your instincts

We have covered red flags in detail, and you are now well-armed with a checklist of signs to look out for.

Take note of them, trust your instincts, and if you feel like you aren't safe, back away. Resist the urge to stay in a situation that makes you uneasy because you don't want to be rude or cause trouble.

You don't have to tell the person why you are no longer available — in fact, with a narcissist, it's better that you don't, as they love confrontation and showdowns. Simply back away, disengage and make it clear that your time and energy are being taken up elsewhere.

3. Don't let yourself get overpowered

Something narcissists are very good at is wearing down their victims. This may be with long, exhausting conversations where you literally cannot escape. It may be by waking you up early or keeping you up late at night so you feel tired and less able to make clear decisions. It may be by keeping you under close scrutiny — watching what you do, asking lots of questions and making lots of comments so you feel self-conscious and targetted.

Be aware of this tendency, and if you feel yourself getting swamped, find a way to free yourself. Get off the phone, go to bed early, go home. Take some time and space to re-energize — a swim, a workout, some meditation or a long walk — and then deal with them. If a narcissist knows that you have clear boundaries around your time and energy, they will move on to someone else.

If it's a good, healthy relationship, they won't mind you taking things slowly.

4. Seek help from a skilled therapist

If you find yourself involved in these relationships again and again, it may be that you need to unpick the deeper reasons with the help of a skilled therapist. This will take time and money, but it may be the best investment you ever make in yourself and your future.

9 Powerful Tips for Developing Unbreakable Self-Love

A tried-and-tested way to protect yourself from narcissists is to develop self-love. This isn't about being egotistical or narcissistic yourself; it's about looking after yourself in the same way you would a good friend or a small child. Here, I've gathered together some simple techniques and ideas to really work on your self-love.

This is something that a narcissist cannot take away from you, and that will keep you safe in the future.

1. Start each day by setting mindful intentions

Intention setting is essentially telling yourself you are worthy of care and love. Start each day with a few moments of mindful breathing and set your intention for the day, which may be something as simple as "Today I am going to take care of myself and show myself love in everything I do because I deserve it."

It may sound strange, but say this — or create a personal message or mantra that works for you — and you will see the benefits. Essentially, a loving mantra or intention sends a signal to your subconscious that you are worthy of love and care that slowly but surely challenges all those negative messages that were given to you by the narcissist.

2. Treat yourself as a friend or small child

If you are feeling down about yourself and can't seem to shake off feelings of low self-esteem, think of yourself as someone else — perhaps a good friend or a small child. What would you do to make him or her feel better? What would you advise? If you were a wise and compassionate friend, what would you tell yourself to feel better? If you were looking after a small child, would you feed her a good meal, run her a warm bath and give her a comforting story in bed?

Writing a letter to yourself is another powerful way to tap into your inner wisdom and kindness. Write down everything you would say to yourself and when you read it back later, you'll be amazed at how powerful your words can be. Keep your letters and read them back to yourself when you need clarity or a bit of support.

3. Acknowledge your feelings

Somethings, simply naming your feelings — *I feel sad*, or *I feel regret* — can be a way of moving through them. We are very good at escaping our feelings in all sorts of ways: numbing out on social media, alcohol, shopping, overeating.

But sometimes taking the time to really feel them — sitting with them, going for a long walk or swim, or writing them down — is the best way to integrate and learn. Instead of always trying to escape, befriend your feelings and you will soon find that they are simply feelings, not a concrete, fixed reality, and they will pass.

4. Treat yourself in healthy ways

Life is here to be enjoyed and savored. If you have found yourself in a relationship with a narcissist, you may have forgotten this. You may be feeling worn out, discouraged and small.

Take back control and treat yourself with acts of kindness and positivity, as you would someone who is recovering from an illness or accident. What are your favorite ways to relax — a funny movie, a holiday, your favorite home-cooked meal in front of the TV, a hot bath or a long swim or walk in the forest?

Make a priority of yourself for a change — do all those things that make you feel good, and leave time to do them regularly.

5.   Meditate

The benefits of meditation are now well known, and regular meditation is a surefire way to boost feelings of calm, happiness and control. Thanks to the internet, it's easy to meditate — just search for guided meditations online, find a quiet space to sit or lie down, and give yourself ten minutes or longer to meditate — you'll soon notice the benefits of increased clarity and joy.

6.   Feel gratitude

It's easy to get ground down by everything that goes wrong, particularly if you have a narcissist in your life reminding you of your every flaw and failure. But research consistently shows that it's feelings of gratitude, not money, wealth or success, that lead to good self-worth.

Take a moment when you remember to think of everything in your life that you feel grateful for — your friends, your health, everything that went well that day, from a small conversation to a quiet moment to reading a good book. Feeling gratitude for the small pleasures of life is the true key to happiness.

7. Look after your body

While focusing on meditation and healthy self-talk will take care of your mind, don't forget about your body. Eating well, drinking lots of water, getting enough sleep and getting some regular exercise — even if it's just a gentle walk or a ten-minute workout video or dancing around the house — are all essential for happiness.

It's so easy nowadays to live in our heads — online or lost in thoughts — while our bodies are neglected. But if you are coming out of a bad relationship, taking care of your physical self is just as important as your emotional wellbeing. And if fact, when your head is a mess, it's sometimes a good idea to go back to basics — food, water, exercise, sleep — as a way of rebuilding your wellbeing.

8. Give back

What selfish people don't realize is that giving to others can reward the giver just as much as the recipient. Taking the time to offer kindness to others is a way of taking care of yourself — volunteer, spend some time playing with a child, raise some money for a good cause, or help a friend out. You'll feel your own happiness rise along with those you are helping.

9. Plan for the future

Once you have taken care of the present moment, spend some time making your future brighter. What can you do today that will make you feel better in a year's time? Think of what you would like to do and where you would like to be and reverse-engineer the process by thinking of what you can do now to get there.

Maybe you need to do some further training or look for some freelance work to fund a dream holiday. Maybe you want to be healthier and fitter, so today you need to push yourself to go for a run. Maybe you want to write a book, so today you set aside an hour to write 500 words.

Keeping a big picture to-do list of what you want your life to look like will guide you in your daily choices and keep you focused on your happiness and life goals.

Chapter 7 - Loving Again

So you've begun to recover from your relationship with a narcissist and you're ready to move forward. Or are you? In this chapter, we'll look at dating and how you can avoid making the same mistakes again with your new partner.

We'll also cover some attitude shifts you need to make so you can enjoy better relationships. We've covered red flags to look out for, and in this chapter, we'll go one step further and look at the early signs that show you've found a good partner. Finally, we'll cover good habits to get a new relationship off to a healthy start.

You can set the terms of a relationship to some extent, and the start is the best time to do it. Ideally, you will have spent some time thinking about relationships and your own patterns, and you will be feeling fresh and energized and ready to venture out into the world of dating again.

What can you do to ensure that your new relationships get off to the very best start? Plenty, as it happens. But first of all, let's look at some things you should definitely avoid.

7 Mistakes to Avoid When You Start Dating Again

If you have been in a relationship with a narcissist, you may still be carrying unhelpful beliefs about what a partner should say and do.

Your judgment can be skewed by spending time with the wrong people. You may also feel as if your confidence has taken a hit. First of all, there's no need to rush straight back out into dating.

Give yourself as much time as you need to recover, using any or all of the ideas I mentioned in the previous chapter. Always bear in mind that you'll need to tread carefully to avoid making the same mistakes again.

Here are some common pitfalls to look out for when you start dating again.

1.   Hiding the truth of who you are

In the the world of dating, it can feel that we need to present ourselves as a shiny package, with interesting hobbies, a great body, and a happy, untroubled face. Don't fall into that trap. Be honest about who you are with everyone you meet, don't feel you have to please or impress, and you will find that the right people come to you.

What if you read this and think — but I don't know who I am? Get curious. Get to know and feel comfortable with yourself, either on your own or with the guidance of a therapist, so when you step out into the world you'll feel more certain of what you're about and less likely to be unsettled by a narcissist.

2.   Rushing in too quickly

As we've seen already, narcissists are adept at moving fast at the start of a new relationship, only for it to fall apart fairly quickly once the initial buzz wears off. Be aware of this tendency when you meet someone and look out for love bombing. Most importantly, take it slow. Don't get drunk and go home with your date that first night, and definitely don't share all your secrets.

Take any outrageous love bombing or commitment talk with a large pinch of salt. If it's meant to be, taking your time won't make a difference. On this note, and it has to be said, don't sleep with someone on the first date if you are thinking it might be a longer-term relationship.

3. Expecting them to commit exclusively

As above, take things slowly. Dating is all about getting to know people, and you can't expect someone to commit just to you on a first date, or even second or third. If someone seems ready to sweep you away and is already talking about an exclusive relationship after three hours in your company, don't fall for it! Someone who falls into infatuation this fast is likely to fall out of it just as quickly, and you are the one who will get burned.

4. Forgetting to enjoy yourself

It's easy to feel like it's all destined to fail after a bad relationship. If you are feeling cynical and bitter, it might be that you're not yet ready or you just haven't found the right person.

You had a bad experience, and that can put you off the whole world of dating in the same way that a bout of food poisoning can put your off the particular food for life. But remember, dating can also be fun. There are — believe it or not — lots of decent, kind, caring people out there who just want to meet someone themselves to spend time with.

You had some bad luck. But it's not your destiny. With some self-care and time to reflect, you will have done some important personal growth that will stand you in good stead when you are ready to try again. Try not to take it too seriously and remember the benefits of mindfulness and gratitude as you move forward. Life is there to be enjoyed, otherwise, what's the point?

An important disclaimer: if you really aren't enjoying life or you feel genuinely anxious and depressed, all the uplifting messages, mindfulness and gratitude in the world might not be enough to make you feel better. Always, always reach out and seek help if you are struggling. See your GP, talk to someone.

5. Seeing a partner as the be-all and end all

You can be perfectly happy single. Oddly, for many people, it's only when they are truly happy on their own and not looking to meet anyone that they actually find someone to commit to.

If you feel that finding someone is an urgent priority in your life, you need to step back a little. Find ways of enjoying time on your own. Spend a whole day on your own doing things you enjoy, make friends with yourself and give yourself the kind of company you would enjoy from someone else.

If you really do feel that finding someone is a matter of urgency, you will only make things harder for yourself. New relationships thrive best in an atmosphere of ease and unhurried fun.

6. Not keeping an open mind

If you have an idea of what your new partner should be like and it's absolutely set in stone, you're going to run into problems. That ideal partner might not exist. Or the ideal partner for you might be nothing like the one you have in your head. My advice is to keep an open mind in general, not just with dating. Be flexible and try new experiences (while always maintaining safe boundaries and looking after yourself).

7. Not trusting your gut

This is probably the most important thing you can do to avoid repeating the same mistake with a relationship. Sure, you might really like someone. They might be attractive, funny, charming and seem to be really into you. It all looks wonderful on the surface as they say and do all the right things.

But how does it feel?

As humans, we are wired to pick up on all sorts of non-verbal signals when interacting with others to work out if they are safe or not. We aren't aware of them a lot of the time, so we can get into the habit of overriding or ignoring these messages from our unconscious if they don't fit in with what we think we want — a relationship, someone to go out with, marriage, babies...
But listening to, and trusting your gut — and then responding to what it is telling you — is one of the smartest things you can do for both your physical and emotional safety.

It may mean being rude and leaving a date or not going home with someone who is incredibly charming and persuasive. It may mean getting told you're rude or difficult.

Don't worry. If you are with someone, and your gut feels tense, or you feel a general sense of uneasiness that you can't quite shake off, believe those messages, and get away as quickly as you can.

If there is one message I hope you will take away from this book, it's this: *Always trust your gut.*

5 Early Signs You've Finally Found a Good Partner

Now that we've discovered what not to do when we start dating again, let's move onto the good stuff: finding someone who is going to make your world a happier place, not turn it upside down. There are many signs you can look out for that will show you you're on the right track with a new partner.

Here are some things to look out for when you start dating that will signal you've found someone you are compatible with.

1. You feel physically at ease in their presence

If you're with someone who is good for you, who isn't going to harm you, you will probably get a warm and easy feeling. The conversation will flow smoothly most of the time. You won't find yourself worrying about what you've said or done, and you will be enjoying yourself.

You'll feel physically safe, comfortable and relaxed. Look for those feelings when you start dating and believe in them, even if the person isn't necessarily your dream partner in every way — sometimes it happens that way.

2. You share common interests and concerns

No matter how attractive someone is or how charming, in a long-term relationship, there needs to be more than just chemistry. If you feel that you share some similar interests and passions, it's a great sign of compatibility. This does not mean someone who agrees with everything you say. It's more about sounding out your world view and knowing pretty quickly that the other person in on the same page.

This isn't to say that you need to be compatible in all ways. In fact, it's great to have some areas where you have absolutely nothing in common. Someone with different interests can teach you about things you've never found interesting before. On the other hand, having interests that your partner doesn't share gives you a sense of space and allows you to maintain a separate identity.

Keep in mind that it's good to enjoy time off in the same way. If you love traveling and your prospective partner does not own a passport, a lifelong relationship may not be in the cards. If they are hugely invested in a hobby — cycling, gaming, running — that doesn't interest you at all, you might need to manage your expectations about their availability.

But if you find that you enjoy at least some of the same things — even if it's as simple as cuddling up on the couch together watching old movies — then chances are you'll enjoy each other's company.

3. They turn up when they say they will

Narcissists are great at running late, creating drama with last-minute cancellations and let-downs. They make a great deal of fuss around the simple act of gracing you with their presence. It's not surprising that being around them can feel hectic and stressful.

What does the opposite experience look like? If someone just shows up on time, looking friendly and relaxed, and you have a nice time together — talking, chatting, walking, seeing a movie or just enjoying a coffee together — you can start to let down your guard and relax.

When you start seeing someone, it should feel like getting to know a friend or work colleague more than a scene straight out of a Hollywood movie. It should feel relaxed, easy, fun. You should feel curious and enlivened, not overwhelmed or swamped with emotion and chemistry. There should be some chemistry, yes, but it shouldn't feel too urgent or over-the-top.

4. They are consistently kind and interested in you

Remember when we looked at intermittent reinforcement? The opposite of this is consistency. If someone is nice to you, but only sometimes, my advice would be to back off. But if someone is consistently pleasant and kind — not over the top, just decent — then you may well be in the presence of a keeper.

Don't waste your time on someone who is only available sometimes, or who gives you just the crumbs of their attention. Generally, if someone likes you, **you know it**. It's not a mystery. If you find yourself wondering about where you stand with someone, it's likely that you aren't their top priority.

5. **You share similar lifestyles**

Sleep, food, exercise, levels of tidiness and daily habits such as reading or exercising — all of these mundane things make up the way you live your life. If you see some compatibility in the small things, then that is a very good sign for your future together. If you walk into someone's house and like the way it looks and feels (rather than feeling impressed, awed, or just slightly nonplussed), you should trust that feeling. A long-term relationship isn't about mindblowing passion and chemistry. It's about enjoying your daily life together, and your daily habits are a big part of this.

On this note, if you want to make your life easier, pay attention to how someone presents themselves and their living space. If they appear uncared for or chaotic, that should give you pause. And if that person is dependent on alcohol or other substances, be aware that they may not have the resources to be a good partner.

8 Great Habits to Start Your New Relationship the Right Way

1. **Slow and steady**

Hold back when you meet someone new. Remember, if they are the one you have all the time in the world to enjoy that fact. If they are not, you should enjoy the relationship for what it is, but also protect yourself so you don't find yourself having to heal and recover from a disastrous relationship.

2. **Treat them as you would like to be treated**

Set the tone for the relationship you would like to have with someone by being that person yourself. Be kind. Be on time. Communicate as clearly as you can. A new relationship is a fresh start, and you can steer it in the right direction by being respectful and positive.

Even when arguments come along — and they will — remember that you have something special between you and you need to look after that, even if you are having a temporary disagreement. It's possible to fight with someone while still remaining respectful and not doing any permanent damage to the bond between you.

If it's meant to be, you'll have set the groundwork for a rich and loving relationship by treating your partner as you would like to be treated.

3. Focus on the other person

To build a strong relationship takes time and effort. It's often the result of many daily interactions, and learning to focus on someone and respond to them is a useful skill for any relationship, not just a romantic one.

To do this, first of all, eliminate distractions. Make time to spend with your partner, switch off screens, listen and focus. Even if you are busy and rushing off in separate directions, eye contact and affection can go a long way in maintaining a healthy and loving connection into the future.

4. Look after yourself

Just because you've met someone new, this doesn't give you an excuse to stop your efforts to heal from your experience with a narcissist. Keep doing all those things you did to recover — talking to a therapist, looking after your physical and mental wellbeing, journaling and spending time alone to rest and recharge. Taking time out to reflect on where the relationship is going and how you are feeling is another way of looking after yourself as you move forward.

Even in the early days, get in the habit of setting aside some personal space, even if you feel like being with them all the time. Give them time to miss you and feel curious about what you've been up to. It's important to give yourself time to enjoy your own company.

5. Don't dwell in the past

Whatever happened with the narcissist, don't let yourself dwell too much on it if it makes you feel bad. Of course, you need to spend some time on it, either alone or with a therapist, but don't live there. When you find yourself ruminating or wondering how the narcissist is going, bring yourself firmly back into the present with self-care or distraction.

On this note, don't assume that all of your future partners are going to let you down. If you have done some work on yourself and reflected on what may have led you to your narcissistic partner, you should be able to avoid carrying this baggage into your new relationship. Give this new person a chance.

6. Remind yourself of how far you have come

If you have been in a relationship with a narcissist, you've been through quite an experience. Always remind yourself of the fact that you got yourself away, you are now safe, and you have a lot to look forward to.

If you find yourself regretting the time you spent with them, remind yourself that you have a whole future ahead of you that they no longer have the power to ruin. You are safe. You deserve to be happy.

7. Don't badmouth the relationship to others

If you are starting out with someone, it's sometimes a good idea to let it grow in its own time, and in private, before you start talking about it too much to others. It's natural to want to share your new relationship with friends, but just be mindful of how much you share. Try to keep some things private. There are a couple of reasons for this.

First, letting others into your new world with this person too quickly, particularly if they prefer you single, can have a negative impact on the new relationship. Secondly, talking about the relationship in detail with others has a way of taking away energy from its growth and opening up the new bond you have formed to the influence of others, who may not have your best interests at heart.

If you aren't sure about how it's going but generally feel OK, talk to your new partner, or your journal, or your therapist. And if you feel suddenly upset, don't go rushing off to badmouth your new partner to your friends. A new relationship is a fragile thing, like a seedling or tiny baby, and you need to treat it will care as it grows stronger.

8. Laugh together

Sharing humor is one of the best ways to relieve stress and bond with your partner. And it's what makes being in a relationship with someone so much fun. So don't forget to laugh, enjoy each other's company, and be silly together.

A final word on finding new love

As you move on from the narcissist, remember to be positive and hopeful for the future, but also realistic. Unfortunately, there are some people out there you need to steer well clear of for your own wellbeing and happiness. But there are also many others who will enrich your life. Ultimately, it's about finding that sweet spot between keeping yourself safe and trusting in those that you meet to do the right thing by you.

If the relationship you've had with a narcissist is good for anything, it's that you have learned how to look after yourself in all sorts of new ways. Believe in your new insights, get out there, and have fun!

Conclusion

Hopefully, in this book, you've found out more about yourself and other people. Use this knowledge to enjoy healthy, satisfying, and joyful relationships. We've been on a journey together, and my sincere wish is that you are feeling energized, educated, and ready to face the future.

Let's take a moment to go over the key points of this book.

First, we looked at the reasons for picking it up in the first place: you suspect you may be in a relationship with a narcissist, and you want to find out more. Or you've come out of a bad relationship and you are now wondering — what happened? You may also want to avoid making the same mistakes again or prevent others from doing so.

I firmly believe that you should know your enemy. And getting to know the narcissist and what makes him or her tick is a tool that will stand you in good stead as you move through life.

We also looked at the key traits of narcissists that make them so easy to spot: primarily, a grandiose sense of self, an unshakeable belief that they are special and uniquely talented. They also have a shameless ability to exploit people, abuse others, and put themselves first.

We also looked at what makes someone a narcissist and how a childhood that combines excessive spoiling with periods of neglect is often what sows the seeds of a narcissistic personality disorder. We saw that despite the strong and overpowering way they present themselves, it's actually very lonely inside the narcissist's head, and they aren't nearly as powerful as they need you to think they are.

We discovered the key warning signs of narcissists, and some of their most common tactics, including gaslighting, love bombing, intermittent reinforcement, and narcissistic rage. The manipulative tactics of narcissists can be quite unsettling to those who are used to more straightforward communication, but once you know and understand them, you are better equipped to deal with them. And most importantly, you've stopped wondering if it's all in your head.

You now know many of the telling phrases that narcissists come out with and what triggers them. You can identify the kinds of people they are attracted to — usually kind and empathic souls who tend to give others the benefit of the doubt. We also looked at how to avoid triggering the narcissist and feeling the full fury of one of their attacks.

Simply put, you can't reason with a narcissist and you can't expect the same reasonable responses from them that you would get from others. Being around a narcissist is not like being around most people — what you need to focus on is primarily protecting yourself, and also managing them so that they can keep themselves under control.

An important point we touched on here is that the narcissist can't change. There is nothing you can do that will improve their behavior, and accepting this and moving forward as best you can is the only sane response.

We then moved on to how this affects their victims. We looked at the damage it can do to you, and why you must leave or disengage for your own wellbeing. Narcissists are very good at manipulating their victims, at holding on tightly when they show signs of leaving and at making a clean break as difficult as possible.

But once you are aware of this, and can keep in mind your own future mental health and wellbeing, you will find within yourself the power to cut the cord for good. The sad thing here is accepting that the narcissist isn't really capable of love or caring relationships, and you need to give up on the hope that you will ever receive what you need from them.

The second part of the book was more active and required more input from you, with lots of techniques and strategies to move forward in your new life, free from this troubling personality.

We looked at how to leave, and the Gray Rock Method as a way of making the narcissist lose interest in you.

We then looked at healing — how to get yourself back to neutral after this disturbing experience, and from there, how to re-energize yourself and move forward with courage, strong self-esteem, and hope.

You discovered all kinds of ways to make yourself stronger and healthier, so that the narcissist can't find a way back in. Mental health options include therapy, meditation, self-love, mantras, and journaling. You can strengthen yourself physically with food, sleep, and exercise. There are so many ways to heal yourself, and I hope you find ones that work for you and enjoy the numerous benefits.

Finally, we looked at breaking the cycle so you don't find yourself in this situation again. We covered what to look for in a relationship, early warning signs, and the signals that you are on the right track to a healthier and more satisfying future.

You deserve to be treated well, you deserve a loving relationship, and I honestly believe that if you do the growth work and take care of yourself, you can find it. Sometimes, a book isn't enough and you need some real-life guidance too: I hope you have the resources and courage to explore further with a trained and compatible therapist, should you need to.

I hope you have enjoyed the journey and found it useful. Narcissists are incredibly frustrating to deal with, and they can do a lot of damage. I wish it weren't the case, but chances are, even if you never have a close relationship with one, you will come across them in your life, your work and your day to day dealings with the world.

Sometimes, you can't simply ignore them. They are widely acknowledged by psychologists as some of the hardest people to treat, so taking the time to read up on them and learn more is a good use of your time and energy. Human nature is fascinating, and you may even get to the point where you can simply enjoy the quirks of a narcissist in your family or working life without being too affected by them.

You now have a whole bunch of effective strategies to deal with narcissists that you can put in place and use as often as you need to (hopefully not at all, but you can't guarantee that!) You know how to look after yourself, how to back away, and how to form healthier and more satisfying relationships with those that will appreciate your presence, time and energy. You know that even if narcissists make it hard for you to leave, you still have the right to do so.

If there is one thing I would like you to take away from this book, it's to **trust your instincts and do whatever you need to to keep safe and happy**. There is no need to suffer with those who aren't good for you, and to give them your time and energy that could be better spent elsewhere.

Narcissists truly are vampires that walk among us, feeding on the good energy of others and at ease with exploiting your kindness and generosity. Don't feel bad about moving away from them, however much they cry and wail. Say no, protect your boundaries, put yourself and your own wellbeing first. You deserve so much more than that from your relationships — and you can have it.